Personalized Curriculum

THROUGH

Excellence in Leadership

Existence is a strange bargain.
Life owes us little; we owe
it everything. The only true
happiness comes from squandering
ourselves for a purpose.

—John Mason Brown

Personalized Curriculum

THROUGH

Excellence in Leadership

O. W. KOPP

The University of Nebraska
Lincoln

DAVID L. ZUFELT

Texas A and I University
Kingsville

Order from

THE INTERSTATE
Printers & Publishers, Inc.

Danville, Illinois 61832

Library of Congress catalog card number: 73-85064

DEDICATION

To those educators who seek
quality education through
purposeful involvement of all
who are concerned with learning.

PREFACE

<u>Personalized Curriculum Through Excellence in Leadership</u> is a work that clarifies the supervisory function in context of instructional and societal change. Throughout the text, "leadership" and "supervisory function" are utilized interchangeably. Part One places a focus upon processes and procedures in curriculum development which hold promise for the revision of all study in consonance with appropriate supervisory behavior. Emphasis is placed on the evolutionary character of change--what by whom. Need for internalization of a systems approach versus "bandwagonism" is stressed.

Part Two provides the reader with specific means of how to use tools of analysis for supervision and interpretation of accumulated data. Some of the topics included are: videotaping, interaction analysis, and self-evaluation. Part Three accents evaluation process. Particular emphasis has been given to evaluation and the process coordinator, heretofore known as the "traditional supervisor."

The Appendixes provide extended and applied information. The Glossary contains the explanation of terms that are used throughout the book.

The last section, "Enrichment Readings," includes selected readings organized by text topic. Each inclusion provides reading enrichment and services as a ready-study reference.

O. W. K.
D. L. Z.

ACKNOWLEDGMENTS

The authors are grateful to Steven M. Fallehy, Oakland, California, and to Merry Ann Whinery Coe and Edith Angus, University of Nebraska at Lincoln, for their technical assistance in the preparation of the manuscript for this book. Also, appreciation is expressed to Janice K. Rogers, Lincoln, for her editorial assistance.

O. W. K.
D. L. Z.

CONTENTS

PART ONE

Process Coordination: The Supervisory Function

Chapter 1

AGENT FOR EDUCATIONAL CHANGE

Central Question

Educational Leadership-Supervision. At a time when leadership and involvement in the decision-making function have become a primary means to articulate a continuous series of learning experiences, supervision remains a misunderstood process in both theory and practice. As a result of this situation, it becomes necessary to delineate the perimeters of the central question facing those supervisors who strive to revise existing courses of study, create and initiate new curricula as well as simultaneously upgrade the quality of instructional competence of tenure, probationary, and first-year faculty. Within this framework, the central question becomes one of determining process, procedures, techniques, and evaluative procedures of curriculum development. Herein lies the greatest promise for revision of all content areas and the four categories identified will be treated in subsequent chapters.

Theory. Combs and Snygg state that "the great human problems of our times press upon us and we need the best possible understanding we can about the nature of man and his behavior."[1] Knowledge of the nature of man and his behavior are fundamental to the central question because expertise in human behaviorism is a prerequisite to implementing and improving total instructional quality. At best, theory, when thoughtfully constructed, provides an analyst-educator with

1. Arthur W. Combs and Donald Snygg. Individual Behavior. New York: Harper and Row, Publishers, Inc., 1959, p. 14.

an approximation concerning the nature of situations. Ultimately, . . ."the best theories must be superseded by something a little better, a little more comprehensive or useful for accomplishing our major purpose. Thus, it should give the professional supervisor courage to achieve the best approximations to the truth of what we are capable in our generation."[2]

Practice. Theory translated into practice becomes a function of, or a coordination of, those forces which affect supervisory behavior. In order to identify those forces which affect supervisory behavior, the analyst-educator utilizes what Postman and Weingarten refer to as the "anthropological perspective." They state, " . . . This perspective allows one to be part of his own culture, at the same time, to be out of it. One views the activities of his own group as would an anthropologist, observing its tribal rituals, its fears, its conceits, its ethnocentrism. In this way, one is able to recognize when reality begins to drift too far away from the grasp of the tribe."[3] An anthropological perspective provides the analyst-educator a clearer picture of reality prior to embarking upon the supervisory function. Tanenbaum and Schmidt suggest that the following forces serve to influence supervisory behavior: "(1) personal value systems; (2) exhibited confidence in subordinates; (3) personal leadership inclinations."[4] Coupled with these forces is the omnipresent factor, the supervisor's interpersonal working relationship with the instructional faculty and administration, which serves as the catalytic agent for successful supervision. The authors further state that teachers who expect strong leadership and then are suddenly required to assume

---

2. Ibid.

3. Neil Postman and Charles Weingarten. Teaching as a Subversive Activity. New York: Delacorte Press, 1969, p. 4.

4. Robert Tanenbaum and Warren H. Schmidt, "How to Choose a Leadership Pattern," Harvard Business Review (March-April, 1958), pp. 95-101.

responsibilities in decision-making often become anxiety-ridden by this experience.[5] This condition exists as a result of their not being consistently involved as active participants in the decision-making function throughout their professional careers beginning with undergraduate preparation.

Fusion of Theory and Practice. In retrospect, emphasis has been placed upon the mechanisms of change. Models, programs, and methods and techniques have been developed and initiated. They have met degrees of success because of the behavioral factors which either act as an agent for progress or set in motion a chain reaction of behavior which modifies or even prevents change from taking place for the improvement of educational offerings at all levels of learning experience. Thus, accurate diagnosis becomes a predetermined requisite when solutions are being sought to the central question. Therefore, human behaviorism is the focal point upon which the quality of supervision rests, regardless of district size or location within the nation.

Separate Subjects or Interdisciplinary Approach

Curriculum Management. Within the evolution of curriculum development during the past three decades, a myriad of approaches to the implementation of the supervisory function and curriculum modification have been developed. These new and varied programs have been initiated; however, a realistic interpretation of the situation must be assessed. Interdisciplinary programs may be desirable, yet fail because of management follow-through and fragmentation. (Figure 1-1.) Prescriptive programs may serve to inhibit rather than expand learning. Figure 1-1 shows a system being restrictive because: (1) a rigid set of directives does not allow for flexibility or consider individual differences and (2) when prescriptive programs become the only vehicles acceptable for learning,

---

5. *Ibid.*, p. 99.

they can and often do become stereotyped and relegated to a routine which eventually undermines individual incentive and the learning process. Thus, prescriptive programs per se serve to structure rather than promote flexible curriculum development and subsequent instruction.

Upon closer examination, prescriptive programs become detached from the total program and cease to be a part of an interrelated series of learning experiences. There is a tendency for them to be detached, a skills function in isolation, and of little applied meaning to the learner. Likewise, this situation becomes a management dilemma for

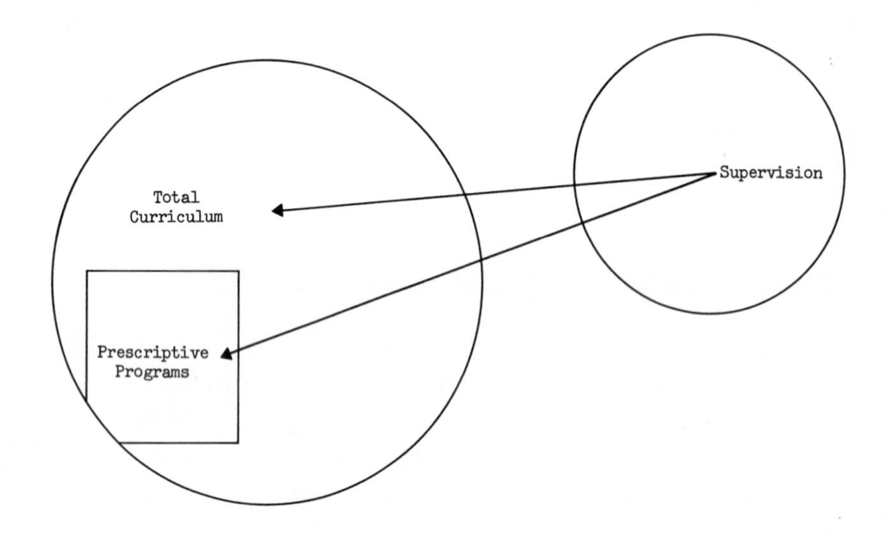

Fig. 1-1

POTENTIAL LEARNING RESTRICTION WITH PRESCRIPTIVE PROGRAMS

the teacher and a source of criticism relative to the supervisory function in terms of expended funds and faculty effort when diminished results are a factor of evaluation. The packaged program may well be likened to placing a square within a circle. Perhaps the packaged program has merely replaced the traditional textbook.

Supervisory Management. Education has witnessed undue expense in time, money, and professional energy at the hands of many an initiator who often becomes a victim of what Koontz refers to as the "management jungle."[6] Theory models solidify into academic exercises unless they can be translated into daily practice within the stresses and complex issues confronting the American public and private schools today.

Koontz continues by suggesting that fundamental problems within the theoretical model become emeshed in a "semantic jungle" as well. Thus, confusion reigns. A salient factor to be considered here is the inability or unwillingness of management to understand each other, and he suggests that in the classification of management theory . . . a few criteria should be utilized:

1. The theory should deal with an area of knowledge and inquiry that is "manageable"; no great advances in knowledge were made as long as man contemplated the whole universe.

2. The theory should be useful in improving practice and tasks and person of the practitioner should not be overlooked.

3. The theory should not be lost in semantics, especially useless jargon not understandable to the practitioner.

4. The theory should give direction and efficiency to research and teaching.

5. The theory must recognize that it is part of a larger universe of knowledge and theory.[7]

---

6. Harold Koontz, "The Management Theory Jungle," The Journal of the Academy of Management, Vol. IV (December, 1961 pp. 174-188. Management theory has been classified into "schools" which include: (1) Management Process School, (2) The Empirical School, (3) The Human Behavior School, (4) The Social System School, (5) The Decision Theory School, and (6) The Mathematical School.

7. Ibid.

Those wrestling with the central question of supervision are confronted with the continual task of the "scientist qua scientist," which calls for a need to be precise when value decisions have to be made.[8] As a result, strategy for supervision should be based upon accurate approximations coupled with value judgments as an outgrowth of human behavior analysis which can be translated into acceptable program options.

Role of Faculty and Administration

Establishment of Role. Establishment of faculty and administrative role is dependent upon an organized body of knowledge. This should include direct experiences which stress the importance of facts and skills. Values and objectives have to be determined. Thus, faculty and administration are compelled to address themselves to the following criteria for assessing present practices and/or directing future improvement in schools:

1. Respect for the worth and dignity of every individual.
2. Equality of opportunity for all children.
3. Encouragement of variability.
4. Faith in man's ability to make rational decisions.
5. Shared responsibility for the common good.
6. Respect for moral and spiritual values and ethical standards of conduct.[9]

The NEA Project on Instruction also indicated the following priorities among educational objectives:

---

8. Ibid.

9. Role of Supervisor and Curriculum Director in a Climate of Change. Washington, D.C.: ASCD, 1965, p. 39.

1. Learning how to learn.

2. Using rational processes.

3. Building competence in basic skills.

4. Developing intellectual and vocational competence.

5. Exploring values in new experiences.

6. Understanding concepts and generalizations.[10]

Therefore, faculty and administration should be concerned with organizational issues and the establishment of priorities. Within this context, "human variabilities demand alternatives."[11] Five organizational issues for faculty and administration to deal with are:

1. The vertical organization of the school should provide for the continuous unbroken upward progression of all learners, with due recognition of the wide variability among them in every aspect of their development. The school organization should, therefore, provide for differentiated rates and means of progression toward achievement of educational goals. Non-grading and multi-grading are promising alternatives to the traditional graded school and should receive careful consideration.

2. Since grouping in terms of ability and/or achievement does little to reduce the overall range of pupil variability with which teachers must deal, this device is not recommended as a general practice. However, selective grouping and regrouping by achievement sometimes are useful.

3. The horizontal organization of the school should permit flexibility in assigning pupils to instructional groups that may range in size from one pupil to as many as a hundred or more. Well-planned cooperation efforts among teachers--efforts such as team teaching should be encouraged.

---

10. Ibid., pp. 39-40.

11. Ibid., p. 46.

4. School organization should be such that it provides opportunity for each student to have a close counseling relationship with competent teachers who know him well. Various forms of organization should be explored. At whatever point specialized personnel are brought into the instructional program, their work should be coordinated with and related to the total program.

5. When the classroom is the unit of organization, teachers should organize learners frequently into smaller groups of varying types and sizes, depending on the educational purposes to be served at a given time.[12]

Once organizational issues have been delineated, priorities and their alternatives can be systematically dealt with if curriculum development and its articulation are to provide an unbroken sequence of learning activities. The priorities might be stated in behavioral terms; however, the faculty and administration have to determine the minimal competencies that a graduate must possess. To do this, professional personnel are forced to find answers to the following questions:

1. What knowledge, values, skills do children and youth in our culture need to learn?

2. Which of these goals can best be achieved by the school?

3. What knowledge, skills, and values can best be taught by the home, the church, and other social institutions?

4. Which learnings require the joint efforts of the school and other agencies?[13]

Much of the present curriculum development has little relevance to current needs of the learner, or if it does, he has difficulty in perceiving the relationship by himself

---

12. Ibid.

13. Ibid., p. 47.

which becomes a function of instruction and curriculum modification. Thus, the leadership function of a supervisor/curriculum director must be one of first assisting faculty and administration at the local level to establish specific educational priorities in behavioral terms. In order to succeed in this task, the following questions need to be answered:

1. Are the staff and public clear about the school's place in the order of things?
2. Has the public, through the local school board, determined the broad aims of the school?
3. Has the professional staff translated these aims into behavioral objectives that indicate priorities?
4. Are the unique nature of each individual and the diversified nature of American life considered when priorities are listed?[14]

Total Involvement Myth. Supervision can become a vital force in educational development if the faculty/administration component systematically deals with the "how" and "when" dimensions. "Rule-of-thumb opinions" often guide and/or dictate decision-making. This haphazard means of problem-solving must cease and be replaced by effective change resulting from problem analysis in consonance with cooperative planning, artistic planning, adaptation of principles, and a willingness to meet new challenges.[15] Three dimensions necessary for intelligent problem-solving involvement are: (1) research--where a selected group establishes the current status; (2) internalization--where involvement in specific terms creates the dynamic situation which allows the group to perceive the work as "our plan"; and (3) satisfaction in attainment--where evidence has been obtained to prove that

---

14. Ibid., p. 48.

15. Ibid.

children profit from their efforts. Thus, differentiated involvement is the means whereby change becomes a reality. Total involvement is a myth indeed.

Functional Application

Interaction of Forces. Continually, faculty and administration are challenged to solve educational problems within the context of eight educational frontiers which "involves the education of individuals in interaction with social forces in the best and worst of times."

1. Helping children and youth to come to grips with international problems of our times.
2. Developing dramatic human relationships among young people of varied races, religions, nationality backgrounds, and social classes.
3. Teaching youth to participate as intelligent citizens on the great human issues of our times.
4. Educating young people for a society in which the unskilled and undereducated are obsolete.
5. Developing young people who are unique individuals, characterized by individual differences and a variety of needs and interests.
6. Helping each and every boy and girl to develop into the best he or she is capable of being.
7. Encouraging young people to cultivate reflective thought, to use maximally the method of intelligence.
8. Answering the fundamental question as to human knowledge, "Knowledge for what?"[16]

---

16. Role of Supervisor and Curriculum Director in a Climate of Change. ASCD Yearbook. Washington, D.C.: Association for Supervision and Curriculum Development, 1965, pp. 19-20.

Supervision or Administration. In the operation of schools today, it is difficult to draw finite distinctions between administrative, supervisory, and leadership functions Although there are some activities which fall clearly in one or another of these categories, there are endless numbers of activities which overlap. Burton and Brueckner state:

> " . . . mere inspection of the typical division between administrative and supervisory duties would indicate that the division can be only an arbitrary one for purposes of discussion. Intimate interrelationship and overlap are inherent and inevitable."

Summary

As an agent of educational change, supervision is continually confronted with the central question of determining processes, procedures, and techniques in curriculum development that hold the greatest promise for curricula revision. Theory and practice applied with an anthropological perspective provide a basis for accurate diagnosis and problem solving. When accurate diagnosis gives way to "opinion," and "rule-of-thumb analysis," new programs fall victim to mismanagement, semantic confusion, and the total involvement myth. This situation can be avoided when values and objectives in consonance with faculty-administration roles are clearly defined. Thus, supervision becomes a viable force for change when systematic analysis replaces haphazard decision-making in curriculum development.

Major Themes

1. The central question concerning the supervisory function is to determine processes, procedures,

---

17. William H. Burton and Leo J. Brueckner. *Supervision: A Social Process*. New York: Appleton-Century-Crofts 1955, p. 98. Reprinted by permission of Prentice-Hall, Inc. Englewood Cliffs, New Jersey.

techniques, and evaluative procedures in curriculum development that hold the greatest promise for revision of all subjects.

2. Thoughtfully constructed theory provides approximations concerning the nature of situations.
3. An anthropological perspective allows an analyst-educator to examine activities and recognize when reality begins to drift from the comprehension of the faculty and administration.
4. Many professional people become anxiety oriented when requested to participate in the decision function and be responsible for the implementation of their decisions.
5. Accurate diagnosis is a primary prerequisite prior to resolving any given problem.
6. Human behaviorism becomes the focus which in turn determines the quality of supervision.
7. New programs have been initiated; however, prescriptive programs tend to become very structured, lacking flexibility and interrelatedness of content.
8. Newly initiated programs have fallen victims of inadequate management and semantic confusion where research, internalization, and satisfaction of a goal are needed.
9. Values and curriculum objectives must be delineated before faculty and administration role can be determined.
10. Haphazard analysis in decision-making has no place in systematic supervision that deals with the "how" and "when" of decision-making.
11. Total involvement in curriculum modification is a myth.
12. Faculty administration and supervisors work interdependently to educate individuals within the interaction of social forces in the "best and worst of times."

Enrichment Readings

Brannen, Ted R., "Changing Business Values," Business Education Forum, Vol. 25 (May, 1971), pp. 31-33.

Brenner, Marcella, "Sunbeams Out of Cucumbers: Why and How Training for Leadership in Education Must Change," Journal of Teacher Education, Vol. 22 (Winter, 1971), pp. 434-442.

Supplementary Readings

Guth, William D., and Renati Tagiuri, "Personal Values and Corporate Strategy," Harvard Business Review, XLIII (September-October, 1965), pp. 123-132.

Katz, M. G., "Educational Innovations Class, Bureaucracy and Schools," Society, Vol. 9 (April, 1972), pp. 53-55.

Kirst, M. W., and D. F. Walker, "Curriculum Planning Analysis of Curriculum Policy-making," Education Digest, Vol. 37 (April, 1972), pp. 28-31.

Rogers, C. R., "Education of Children, Can Schools Grow Persons?" Education Digest, Vol. 37 (April, 1972), pp. 20-21.

Taylor, A. J., "Teaching Machines, Those Magnificent Men and Their Teaching Machines," Education Digest, Vol. 37 (April, 1972), pp. 13-16.

West, C. P., "First Priority for Faculty," Liberal Education, Vol. 57 (December, 1971), pp. 521-528.

Chapter 2

RELATION OF FACULTY AND ADMINISTRATION TO CONCEPTUAL MODIFICATION

The Importance of Responsible Supervisory Behavior

Personnel Affect the Climate of Supervisory Function. The role of the supervisor is basically one of a service function. In this role, the supervisor holds the key to the direction, quality, and success of program development at the local level. A prerequisite to the initiation of any new program is that a clear understanding of the objectives and goals be agreed upon by the teacher, principal, central administration, and the supervisor. With this understanding, the supervisor can begin to work toward moving the program ahead. Any program will correlate directly with the knowledge of curriculum which the supervisor has concerning the intended project and his effectiveness in working with people.

Commitment to Service and Curricula Improvement. The concept of supervisory role becomes a primary consideration because the assumed role reflects professional attitudes which are translated into observable behavior in the performance of his assumed duties. Service to the school system and a commitment to carry out immediate, intermediate, and long-range objectives of the district become the basis upon which supervisory behavior is interpreted and ultimately evaluated. Curriculum development and instruction are viewed as being inseparable. Fundamental to the service commitment is the internalization of the belief that a "*course of study*" is not something done separately and apart by a "*curriculum specialist*" who then initiates it into the schools where it is implemented by an "*instructional specialist*." Should such a separation exist, the supervisory personnel fail to recognize that a process of curriculum development involves a wide range of activities from clarification of the instructional objectives to the in-service education of the faculty.[1]

Supervision: A Many-Titled and Activity-Oriented Function. Today, when there is a trend for precision of performance criteria within curriculum development, the position and supervisory function remain a nebulous definition throughout the nation. A supervisor, as traditionally known to the professional community, may be one of the following personnel: (1) assistant superintendent, (2) director, (3) coordinator, (4) supervisor, or (5) consultant. Usually, each person is responsible for one or more of the following activities which directly or indirectly affects the instructional function and serves to either support or diminish the impact of implemented educational objectives at the local district level. These activities are: (1) planning, (2) administration, (3) supervision, (4) curriculum development, (5) demonstration teacher, and (6) research.[2] The curriculum component is a function of systematic articulation of the aforementioned six elements of supervision. Successful implementation of this interrelated set of activities is dependent upon the role expectation set for the supervisor. Regrettably, it matters not so much what a supervisor actually does, but rather what significant contributions others think he can make.

Categories of Behavior. Sweitzer's investigation of supervisory effectiveness relative to improving instructional programming utilized five general categories of supervisory behavior: (1) authority centered, (2) inner centered, (3) work group oriented, (4) individual centered, and (5) other centered.[3] Upon examination of these five categories,

---

1. William H. Burton and Leo J. Brueckner. Supervision: A Social Process. New York: Appleton-Century-Crofts, 1955, pp. 11-13.

2. William H. Lucio and John D. McNeil. Supervision: A Synthesis of Thought and Action. New York: McGraw-Hill Book Company, 1962, pp. 23-24.

3. Robert E. Sweitzer. The Fulfillment of Role-expectations and Teacher Morale. Ph.D. Dissertation. University of Chicago, 1957, pp. 2-3.

supervisory self-concept is revealed. This wide range of behavior, from an authority centeredness to other centeredness, demonstrates the need for clarification of the supervisor's role. Those engaged in the act of supervision should be reminded that as parameters of a position are defined, understood, and accepted by all affected personnel, the supervisor's behavior more naturally moves toward the other centered orientation.

Conversely, those working in loosely defined positions and functions, who perceive themselves as threatened personnel and proliferate Parkinson's Law, produce a situation whereby a supervisor becomes authority oriented--literally reigning. At the same time, the "other oriented" personnel who believe in total involvement on the part of the faculty, in a literal sense, represent potential management chaos. Hence, supervisory personality coupled with management expertise become factors that ultimately serve to support or undermine the supervisory function.

Teacher Reaction to Supervisory Group Processes. For many a supervisor, leadership and manipulation of personnel are perceived as one and the same. Manipulation eventually is viewed as a deceptive tactic to control group process. Kimball Wiles provided insight into this issue which has caused the supervisory function to become limited relative to improving curriculum in both the public and parochial schools. Wiles listed the following teacher reactions to group process under the leadership of supervisors:

1. Time was wasted in too many committees.
2. Teachers disliked the proliferation of committees.
3. Teachers deplored the shallow results of committee efforts.
4. Progress was often subject to the least common denominator in group work.
5. Petty differences among members tended to crowd out work on critical problems.

6. Vested interests of individuals prevented group decisions for needed change.

7. Confusion of role, functions, and responsibilities occurred.

8. Principals were unable to cope with their roles as curriculum leaders.

9. Supervisors were assigned to inconsequential tasks and were frustrated by their inability to effect curriculum and instruction to any great extent.[4]

To overcome the preceding criticisms, some basic guides for positive results must be explored. The following bench marks are worthy of consideration:

1. Those persons who are receptive to the particular project should become involved.
2. All members of a faculty will not be interested in the same project. This fact should be recognized, and the faculty should be provided with options for participation.
3. The interested faculty should thoroughly research the potential of the proposed project.
4. As the working group internalize the project, it becomes their project, and effectiveness of the project is on the way to becoming a reality.
5. As the project is implemented and positive results are observed, satisfaction in attaining a goal helps mark the project a success.

Four Crucial Behavioral Factors That Serve to Thwart the Supervisory Function. First, the local building principal is regarded professionally as the curriculum leader; yet, many instructional personnel perceive him as being unable to fulfill this role without outside assistance. With our rapid expansion in the educational sector, the need for administrative personnel has been acute. Because of this need

---

4. Kimball Wiles. Supervision for Better Schools, 3rd ed. Englewood Cliffs, New Jersey: Prentice-Hall, Inc., 1964, Ch. 4.

certification requirements have only too often been met without bringing a depth of professional experience to the position. It is also true that too often a principal has been primarily associated with non-instructional assignments. Hence, the opportunity to keep informed about curriculum development and instructional practice in terms of recent developments may be somewhat limited. Reflecting upon the central question, one must consider whether a building principal should exercise supervision relative to curriculum development. It would seem that a building principal's role is, indeed, chiefly one of facilitating the learning process, an important facet of curriculum development. The principal must be a partner in curriculum development; he need not play the leadership role.

Second, vested interests, whether faculty, administration, supervisor, or lay board oriented, act as an _extra-legal force_ which restricts the supervision program. This aspect of behavior assumes that the vested interest is correct and not subject to question worthy of implementation, regardless of _residual consequences_.

In this situation, the initiator of the vested interest seldom is willing to be _accountable_ for the error of his judgment. Likewise, he may not be able to comprehend the additional damage perpetrated. Persons with _hidden agendas_ should not always be interpreted as being negative. However, when vested interests become an act of self-aggrandizement or a manifestation of personal and political bias at the expense of total program objectives, an immoral act has been committed by the self-oriented personnel. To overcome this ever-present influence, personnel of principle and integrity, those who are uncompromising relative to the service commitment and above personality differences, can exert leadership to define the real issues and work toward an acceptable solution. Otherwise, once again, children are the victims. Ultimately, the community and nation are poorer because of indefensible decision-making by irresponsible behavior of an influential few among the professional corps.

Third, decisions are made by the majority rather than a _consensus_ being sought. The notion still exists that the majority is "right," which is a basic false assumption. It may be that a majority of personnel is uninformed, and then, the majority has determined a decision based upon ignorance without knowing the difference. Before final decisions are arrived at, a consensus provides a means whereby one can evaluate whether or not additional data or clarification needs to be presented as a result of reactions and inquiry. Utilization of consensus provides a procedural alternative prior to decisions which better insures that final decisions are based upon an intelligent analysis of thorough data, whereas, relying upon simple majority decisions suggests vested interests or a coalition effort comprises a majority. Thus, the supervisory function is reduced to a level of decision function unworthy of intelligent and dedicated professional educator analysts.

Fourth, words are used to prevent thinking. Strange as it may seem, word selection, coupled with _delivery type_, can serve to curtail thinking by those participating in a supervisory program. An example is the supervisor who was formerly a primary classroom teacher, who, when promoted to a supervisory position, addresses faculty gatherings in a manner befitting a class of primary children. In contrast, the self-centered semantic "hot shot" steeped in professional jargon sets out to impress the listener. He sounds learned but says next to nothing. A technical specialist often assumes that those whom he is assisting have more technical knowledge than actually is the case. This assumption tends to place faculty on the defensive. In each of these three situations, well-meaning personnel committed to the service function of supervision have diminished their effectiveness with inappropriate word choice and delivery.

Thinking per se was not prevented, but rechannelled. Thinking by the listener-receiver focused upon the interpreted arrogance of the supervisor rather than thinking with him in terms of what was being said. The spoken word, fundamental to articulate communication, becomes an agent of confusion and misunderstanding of intended behavior on the part of the supervisor which becomes a barrier to intra-faculty cooperation. This phenomenon can coalesce to resist the efforts of the best organized supervisory programs.

Four crucial components of the supervisory function are: (1) the principal who has difficulty in his curriculum leadership role, (2) vested interests, (3) decisions made by the majority avoiding the consensus prior to decision-making, and (4) words which cause a rechannelling of thinking join to form a matrix which eclipses the most definitive supervision program. If a building principal is unable to cope with his role as an educational leader, it is but a matter of time until the remaining elements will appear as _dysfunctions_ serving to scuttle any potentially successful supervisory activity.

Administration Attitude Reflects Quality of Educational Change

Attitude and the Supervisory Activity. Earlier in this work, Sweitzer's role expectation categories were introduced.[5] Depending upon the category placement, an administrator-supervisor exhibits his capacity to delegate meaningful authority and achieve desired accountability. In effect, the supervisory activities conceivably range from inconsequential tasks to sustaining a systematically coordinated supervisory program. Administrative attitude can either enhance or undermine cooperation.

Supervision has not escaped the effect of Parkinson's Law, and again illustrates a function of administrative attitude which serves to impede change as well as daily administrative functions.

---

5. Sweitzer, _op. cit._, pp. 2-3. General categories include: (1) authority centered, (2) inner directed, (3) work group oriented, (4) individual centered, and (5) other directed.

> Applying this law to school administration, picture a school supervisor who feels overworked. Because of this feeling, he may resign, or halve his work with a colleague, or demand the assistance of two subordinates. Rather than lose pension rights or bring a rival for promotion, Parkinson's Law predicts he will demand the subordinates. Two are necessary for status reasons and to keep each other in order in fear of the other's promotion. Parkinson gives full account of the second force by which several officials do what one did before, making so much work for each other that all are fully occupied and the original supervisor is working harder than ever.[6]

All professional personnel involved in developing a means to create and modify curriculum should be mindful of Parkinson's Law because it serves to complicate rather than bring about functional efficiency. When the service commitment in supervision is accepted, reflected attitudes will then concern themselves with providing instructional personnel with experiences with which to exert leadership as well as develop leadership competencies.

Generalizations Concerning Curriculum Leadership. Dispersed opportunities for leadership among the faculty of school systems should be *modus operandi* within the supervisory function. Thus, the following generalizations can be made:

1. Curriculum leaders should accept present opportunities to decentralize leadership within schools, and should plan for reorganizing schools so that leadership emerges more readily.

2. Curriculum leaders should show respect for individual differences among staff members so that competencies may emerge and enrich the program.

3. Curriculum leaders should expect to serve as consultants and guides rather than merely directors.

---

6. Northcote Parkinson. *Parkinson's Law and Other Studies in Administration*. Boston: Houghton Mifflin Company, 1957, pp. 3-4.

4. Curriculum leaders should encourage the use of problem-solving methods in dealing with curriculum problems.

5. Curriculum leaders should prepare and help operate plans for training other curriculum leaders.[7]

Curriculum Leadership Competencies. In order to fulfill the delimited generalizations suggested by the ASCD, Doll lists competencies which curriculum leaders must be able to demonstrate if they are going to accomplish their professional assignments. These competencies are:

1. Practising good human relations;
2. Adhering to principles to human growth and development;
3. Knowing, when, where, and under what conditions curriculum change occurs;
4. Using group process techniques;
5. Relating quickly to other people;
6. Developing the creative abilities of other people;
7. Inventing new plans for organizing personnel and facilities;
8. Knowing how to solve educational problems;
9. Seeing themselves as others see them.[8]

Attitudes of administrators committed to perceiving supervisory activities as a service function are more amenable to faculty development within the context of a planned supervision program. Therefore, successful attitudinal sets become an outcome of the perceived need to decentralize leader-

---

7. Association for Supervision and Curriculum Development. Action for Curriculum Improvement (1951 Yearbook). Washington, D.C.: The Association, 1951, p. 187.

8. Donald C. Doll. Curriculum Improvement: Decision-Making Process. Boston: Allyn and Bacon, Inc., 1968, pp. 174-175.

ship so that specific contributions are in consonance with local school district objectives.

Faculty-Administration Behavior in Decision-Making

Total Involvement a Misnomer. Throughout the evolution of the supervisory function, those concerned with group dynamics have been educated to believe that effective curriculum development is a result of total involvement. Mass involvement is an incomprehensible effort because each member of any given faculty can not conceivably contribute equally to all projects in curriculum development. Effective curriculum development results from utilizing professional expertise of individual personnel. This specialized individual contribution insures a maximum of quality proportionate to input of effort; thus, integrity in curriculum development is maintained.

Excellence: A Realistic Outgrowth of Decision-Making. Kopp and Zufelt state:

> Excellence in its current application emphasizes the individual who desires knowledge and is motivated to achieve that goal. It is the attitude of wanting to aspire to the level of greatest satisfaction in all human occupational and personal activity. Thus, by inference, an egalitarian and excellent society would evolve when its educational opportunities to each of its citizens according to ability and self-motivation and when purposeful attention to individual differences enables each citizen to realize excellence of self.[9]

When service commitment in supervision, intelligent decision-making, and excellence as a realistic goal of learning experience combine to influence curriculum develop-

---

9. O. W. Kopp and David L. Zufelt. Personalized Curriculum: Method and Design. Columbus, Ohio: Charles E. Merrill Publishing Co., 1971, p. 7.

ment, faculty-administration behavior is at a high professional level of operation.

Planning for Excellence in Decision-Making. Planning must take into consideration society, the learner, and organized knowledge as faculties participate in the problem-solving process. The following must be given careful consideration in all facets of planning:

1. That the school reflect the demands of society.
2. That the schools plan curricula to fill the societal demands, e.g., drug programs.
3. That the myth of total involvement poses a challenge to supervisory leadership.
4. That planning for change must identify the operational and realistic frame of reference within which the program is to be implemented.
5. That totally unrealistic program objectives can thwart faculties and impede progress.

Establishing priorities is the logical consideration when developing objectives and attempting to fulfill immediate, intermediate, and long-range goals of any designated school district.

Summary

Acceptable professional behavior of a supervisor as interpreted by instructional and administrative personnel is a primary factor in initiating and maintaining a systematic program designed to improve curriculum at the local school-district level. Yet, acceptable behavior must be coupled with a service-commitment philosophy in order to have a designed program become functional. The trend for job description within the profession has not applied to supervision because the supervisory function remains defined under many titles. Within this frame of reference, behavior types signify an attitude toward this professional position.

Supervisory programs have been severely criticized by the instructional personnel, primarily in the areas of wasting time, manipulating tactics, and proliferating committee work, which expends great amounts of effort only to realize little change with reference to implemented action on the part of administration. Because many building principals continue to be responsible for curriculum leadership, they need the assistance of qualified supervisory personnel. Assuming that expertise is desirable, each school district should provide opportunities for leadership competencies to be developed by individual faculty members.

All personnel cannot make an equal contribution in curriculum development projects. The concept of total involvement is a misnomer. A service commitment is essential if supervisory activities are to make a viable contribution to curriculum development which serves to support an egalitarian concept of excellence. Planning for excellence brings about higher levels of decision resolution when attempting to meet immediate, intermediate, and long-range educational objectives at the local school-district level.

Major Themes

1. Supervisory behavior determines the overall success of any supervisory program.
2. Successful supervisory activities are based upon a commitment of service.
3. Supervisory functions are undertaken by personnel with many titles and are activity oriented.
4. The behavioral category in which a supervisor may be placed provides insight into self-concept.
5. Group processes in supervisory activities are critically evaluated by instructional personnel.
6. Instructional personnel tend to tolerate supervisory programs rather than to sincerely participate in them.
7. Parkinson's Law is operative in public and private school supervision.

8. Curriculum leaders should provide activities whereby the faculty can learn to acquire leadership competencies.
9. Total involvement in curriculum development by each faculty member is a misnomer.
10. An egalitarian concept of excellence is a realistic outgrowth of intelligent decision-making at the local district level.
11. Planning by professional personnel should focus upon the learner.
12. Planning for excellence causes priorities to be identified.

Enrichment Readings

Allen, Rowanneta S., "Role and Function of Supervisors and Curriculum Workers," Educational Leadership, Vol. 23 (January, 1966), pp. 330-333.

Cross, Ray, "The Principal as a Counterpuncher," National Elementary Principal, Vol. 51 (October, 1971), pp. 26-29.

Greig, James, and Robert R. Lee, "Cooperative Administration," National Elementary Principal, Vol. 44 (January, 1965), pp. 71-76.

St. Mary, Maurice E., "The Administrative Team in Supervision," National Elementary Principal, Vol. 45 (April, 1966), pp. 59-61.

Supplementary Readings

Amidon, Edmund J., Kathleen M. Kies, and Anthony T. Palise, "Group Supervision: A Technique for Improving Teaching Behavior," National Elementary Principal, Vol. 45 (April, 1966), pp. 54-58.

Belasco, James A., and Joseph A. Alutto, "Decisional Participation and Teacher Satisfaction," Educational Administration Quarterly, Vol. VIII (Winter, 1972), pp. 44-58.

Conner, Forest E., "Challenge for School Administrators," National Elementary Principal, Vol. 51 (October, 1971), pp. 74-75.

Eash, Maurice J., "Preparatory Programs for Supervisors," Educational Leadership, Vol. 23 (February, 1966), pp. 358-362.

Erikson, D. A., "Changes in the Principalships: Cause for Jubilation or Despair?" National Elementary Principal, Vol. 44 (April, 1965), pp. 16-20.

Gifford, Beverly, "New Path to Educational Leadership: National Program for Educational Leadership (NPEL)," American Education, Vol. VII (December, 1971), pp. 9-12.

Hill, John, and William R. Martin, "Training for Educational Decision Making," Journal of Teacher Education, Vol. 22 (Winter, 1971), pp. 443-447.

Lipham, James M., "Organizational Character of Education," Review of Educational Research, Vol. 34 (October, 1964), pp. 443-444.

Reasoner, Robert W., and Harvey R. Wall, "Developing Staff Interaction in Team Teaching," National Elementary Principal, Vol. XLIV (January, 1965), pp. 84-86.

Usery, Mary Lou, "Supervision: Focus on Thinking," Educational Leadership, Vol. 23 (December, 1965), pp. 225-229.

Chapter 3

ELEMENTS OF CHANGE WHICH INSURE CONTINUOUS INSTRUCTIONAL IMPROVEMENT

System for Change Defined

Change. Change for the mass usually is acceptable so long as it affects someone else. Change to others is associated with fad and fashion, a galaxy of expensive programs which blaze with impression only to fizzle and sputter into oblivion like a sparkler on the Fourth of July. Yet many more perceive change as a threat to their professional security. All of these attitudes apply to supervisory personnel and their applied functions. Pragmatically, change is a universal constant which can be predictable when planned for by foresightful educators. Therefore, change per se is not in question, but the means by which change is managed is in need of examination.

The Mean in Conflict with the Result. The age-old conflict of means justifying the ends moves front and center in this issue. First, any selected means to effect change without systematic analysis and projected planning is unacceptable. This approach is characteristic of amoeba orientation--blurping along precipitously, always a victim of sordid pressures of hidden agendas. When any means becomes justifiable without being based upon professional analysis, educational activity filters down to a residue of keeping school. Second, egocentric motivation often becomes a means of promoting change. In effect, the initiation syndrome becomes a logistical vehicle for personal aggrandizement. This all too familiar situation brings into focus a facet of the central question confronting educational units from the neighborhood schools to include an entire public and/or private school system.[1] Those responsible for supervision must answer this gnawing question, "Is our school system leadership using its position as a means of professional advancement within the so-called educational aspirations of the community for which it serves?" Thus, a society such as ours--technologically oriented, urban centered, and wrestling with stockpiled knowledge awaiting assimilation into the mainstream of instruction--is in need of stable leadership. The required leadership must be able to guide mass education at all levels of learning. Therefore, the present dilemma is one of coordinating efficient management practice. Third, an attitude of professional service which once permeated the profession two or more decades ago seems to have diminished, where ideals are now relegated to the neophyte who in three to five years joins the rank and file of the tenured syndrome in order to survive in a quagmire of inept leadership.[2] Meaningful change can never be brought about by the hypocritical opportunist. Finally, how change is brought about becomes the basic issue. Fundamental to every element of change is a planned procedure involvement including: (1) personnel, (2) priorities, and (3) phase-in rate of program adoption and modification.

Evolution or Revolution. Change for long-range effort becomes a function of evolution. Carry-over into the cultural mainstream through national acceptance of a tested method, technique, or theory may take several decades.[3]

---

1. The central question becomes one of determing processes, procedures, techniques, and evaluative procedures of curriculum development.

2. Low birth rate during the decade 1930-1940 leaves the nations in the decade 1970-1980 without a large reservoir of potential leadership, which illustrates how the leadership void, in part, came into being.

3. Acceptance of change varies with reference to the continuously planned public relations program inclusive of in-service education for the taxpaying public and endowing institutions.

Educational change defies flamboyancy and harshness of revolution. Like learning, change is an integrating process, unobtrusive but persistent in its evolutionary conquest of the status quo. Motivated intent coupled with time becomes a pillar upon which the potential for meaningful change rests.

Establishing a Priority of Need

Priority. The determination of priority is a process which can be determined when educational leadership has a defined and operational philosophy of education. Priorities relative to curriculum development must continually be in consonance with the long-range objectives of a system's educational philosophy. Elements of priority selection take into consideration the locale's values and traditions; however, establishing a priority should be the result of determining what a learner needs to know in the skills area and academic or technical knowledge. All too often, the lack of systematic orderliness in priority selection serves to thwart realistic change. In this decade, procrastinating leadership that is unwilling to establish priorities relative to curriculum development joins those who tenaciously keep up with yesterday.

Need. Curricula need is elusive because it changes in kind and emphasis continually. As a result, need becomes a function of programming which allows a student to select courses of study. These courses of study should prepare an individual for a professional task as well as add to his general knowledge. Need, then, becomes two segments of a whole where its characteristics are both personal and institutional in orientation. Thus, allowance must be made for the inclusion of those studies which systematically guide the learner through a sequence of experiences which provide for personal identification.

A Professional Decision. Establishing a priority of need cannot be superimposed upon a faculty or tax-paying public. It is a professional decision based upon gathered data and consultation with significant personnel. Regardless of the scope of involvement, a professional decision must be made ultimately by an administrative officer who is accountable to the Board of Education. The inclusion of fads, which tend to be associated with short-lived programming, should be avoided. When fad and fashion enter the decision process, leadership becomes suspected of creating an impression in contrast to providing for purposeful curriculum development. Thus, the establishment of a priority of need is decision resulting from accurate data analysis in terms of the school system's educational philosophy and long-range planning--a professional decision.

Objectives of a Change System

Specific Objectives. The objectives of a change system are twofold: (1) to provide for increased relevance within the curriculum and (2) to prepare learners for positions in a world of work that currently does not exist. These two behavioral objectives become the central issue of priority determination. Priority centers in the creation of criterion-performance objectives that achieve the intended twofold purpose. At the same time, this issue is compounded by the fact that much of what is presented to children and adults by teachers is not worth knowing. Data continues to be memorized, only to be forgotten at the termination of the last test, where many complete an academic sequence to be prepared for nothing. At the eleventh hour, a student realizes he may be as ignorant as the day he began his selected course of study. Thus, the objectives of change seek to humanize and personalize the learning process where foresightful leadership can exercise an effective role in assisting teachers to bring about those learning experiences which create a worthy product rather than one that must undergo continual rehabilitation.

Increased Relevance. Change and priority, when determined by professional decision-making, enhance the potential for increased relevance in the curriculum. Relevance is perceived when a learner experiences assistance in the examination of his basic assumptions about society and its improvements. This examination deals with values and social policies.[4] The seeking of self-identity seems to be more worthy than minority programs emphasizing culture and pride. As a result, historical and cultural studies have increased relevance when they assist in predicting the future or to make the transition.[5]

Preparation and the Learner. New answers are needed for the central question of supervision.[6] To date, human resource has been overshadowed by industrial resource capability. Realistically, educated man is the central resource where the total educated mass becomes the capital of society. With this as a frame of reference, selection of educational objectives to prepare the learner for positions that do not exist can become a reality.[7]

Supervision as a process has a definite role to assume in the achievement of the objectives of change. Not unlike a business enterprise, clearly defined responsibility, based upon accurately analyzed data in consonance with long-range planning, must direct educational leadership. The issues to be solved are fundamental to any management enterprise. They become complex and unmanageable when decisions lose focus upon the learner and become subservient to the games that people play.

---

4. Lawrence E. Metcalf and Maurice P. Hunt, "Relevance and the Curriculum," Phi Delta Kappan (March, 1970), p. 360.

5. Ibid. p. 361. Significant questions to be answered are: (1) What kind of person am I now? (2) What kind of person will I become if present habits and trends persist? (3) What kind of person would I like to become? (4) What does one do about tendencies and preferences that conflict?"

6. See footnote no. 1, this chapter.

7. Glen Hass, "Who Should Plan the Curriculum?," Educational Leadership, XIX, No. 1 (October, 1961), p. 3.

Activities to Achieve and Implement Objectives

A Realistic Approach. Assuming supervisory leadership is seriously intent upon enacting the objectives of change, a behavior analysis of the school principal must be made. The local building principal has been selected because in the majority of cases he exercises supervisory activities concerning curriculum within the attendance unit. The authors have previously stated that building principals need not exercise this leadership; however, the fact remains, they do. Thus, the student of supervision must examine current leadership behavior before substituting means whereby effective realization of objectives can be sustained.

Games That Principals May Play. Demsch and Muller succinctly pinpoint a system of games and options that are played by building principals at all levels of instruction throughout the nation. Five possible reasons for such behavior are suggested:

1. possible threats to his status in the school system.

2. uncertainty about his line authority.

3. hesitation about how, when, and where to use his authority.

4. a need to be liked and accepted.

5. a need to express feelings of displayed hostility within the complex school structure.[8]

The games played by the principal are described by Demsch and Muller as:

1. I'm Governed by Rules and Regulations

2. Don't Rock the Boat

---

8. Berthold Demsch and Don Muller, "Games That Principals Shouldn't Play," Clearing House, XLV (April, 1971), pp. 473-474.

3. Cross Examination--Your Witness

4. Let's Form a Committee.[9]

In each of these games, the key to the behavioral reaction is one of integrity needed to make decisions and coordinate a matrix of conflicting factors for which he must be accountable. If leadership does not accept its strengths and limitations and seek to work cooperatively with the faculty, the teachers, pupils, and tax-paying community continue to participate in an "unending masquerade."

Planning for Implementing Objectives. Supervisory leadership must accept an earlier premise that total involvement serves to frustrate rather than resolve issues. Hence, the activity of planning becomes primary to success. All personnel and lay persons who register vested interest should be consulted prior to operational program design. Articulate planning can be overstressed. Problems at the local school level, regardless of size, can be traced back to the absence of analytical foresightful planning. Within this setting, alternatives have to be considered. Without alternatives, basic planning is diminished relative to projected objectives.

Adaptability. Administrative personality lurks within the game set; however, an able supervisory-oriented administrator who has devised a plan acceptable to the active participants may not succeed because of inflexible management. Broudy reminds us that ". . . once technology makes social justice possible, we cannot get by with good intentions."[10] Likewise, the same is true for objectives of change--adaptability is a mandate to be honored.

Specific Activities. Guidelines for any activity should stress continuity of purpose and personnel involvement whereby each participant can recognize the constructive effect of his input and avoid manipulation of faculty and staff. When the

---

9. Ibid.

10. Harry S. Broudy, "Art, Science, and New Values," Phi Delta Kappan (November, 1967), p. 117.

supervisory leadership is suspected of "game playing" and "manipulation," two aspects of administrative behavior most often criticized by the instructional staff, the whole program of supervision is bogged down in a hopeless morass of suspicion. A realistic approach to specific activities for the supervisor can be found in Appendix A.

Evaluation

Basis for Evaluation. Rising above personality, the behavioral objectives developed which represent the desired outcomes of curriculum development should be the basis for evaluation of pupil success. Behavioral objectives can be both pupil and teacher oriented. Evaluation in relation to supervision is a continuous activity which is designed to increase both student and teacher competence. Elements of desirable instruction can be delineated, and they must be if the profession is to maintain and improve instructional competence.[11]

The Evaluator. Because accountability has become a sensitive area in education, the rank and file of both the students and teachers are concerned with who and what instruments will be utilized for continuous evaluation. Behavioral objectives which include criterion performance allow for personalized learning which takes into account differential rates of learning. For the student, the criteria set for in the objectives state a level of acceptance which is mentored by his instructor/classroom teacher. Therefore, it is logical that an assigned person representing the supervisory staff would be provided with the authority to develop, administer, interpret, and counsel staff with reference to the evaluation of instructional performance. No different than industry,

---

11. Evaluation scales were designed by Flanders and Amidon; Harris and McKnight represent two means by which teachers can be evaluated. Harris and McKnight include the use of the VTR. These evaluation tools have relevance when each is adapted for an intended use at the local district level.

the professional educator has to be accountable for his performance in consonance with his professional responsibility. The educator at all levels of instruction, administration, and supervision no longer has immunity from evaluation. (Appendix B.)

Summary

Change is a universal constant and it must be continuously planned for by supervisory leadership. The challenge is one of successfully managing conflicting goals to achieve an acceptable philosophy of education whereby change supports the determination of processes, procedures, techniques, and curriculum development. A supervisor must accept the fact that change is a function of evolution rather than revolution.

Priority determination in terms of need must always be a professional decision. As a result, increased relevance in the curriculum and preparation of learners for positions currently not in existence, which represent the objectives of change, can be realized.

A factor to be contended with remains the professional behavior of the building principal/supervisor. Playing "games" and resorting to "faculty manipulation" serve to undermine effective change. When implementing programs for change, articulate planning and flexible adaptability, free from faculty suspicion, aid in sustaining change. The evaluation of change should be continuous, based upon behavioral objectives in terms of both course requirements and professional-instructional responsibilities.

Major Themes

1. Change is a universal constant which can be predictable when planned for by foresighted educators.
2. The means by which change is managed is the central issue.

3. Effective change is the result of an evolutionary process.
4. Establishing a priority of need is fundamental to change.
5. Priority selection must be a professional decision.
6. The objectives of change center upon increased relevance within the curriculum and preparation of learners to assume positions currently non-existent.
7. Principals/supervisory personnel may participate in a "never-ending masquerade" which serves to undermine change.
8. Planning and adaptability are fundamental to implementing the objectives of change.
9. Evaluation of designed change should be a continuous activity based upon criterion-performance objectives, both pupil and teacher oriented.

Enrichment Readings

Buell, Clayton E., "Guidelines for Curriculum Development," Educational Leadership, Vol. II (December, 1968), pp. 293-297.

Telfer, Richard G., "Staff Involvement Key to Curriculum Improvement," Clearing House, Vol. 43 (May, 1969), pp. 539-542.

Supplementary Readings

Bushnell, David S., "A Systematic Strategy for School Renewal," Educational Technology, Vol. XII (February, 1972), pp. 27-33.

Eberle, Robert, "Have You Met Any 'Darn Fools' Today?" Contemporary Education, Vol. XLIII (January, 1972), pp. 176-177.

Harris, Ben M., "New Leadership and New Responsibilities for Human Involvement," Educational Leadership, Vol. 26 (May, 1969), pp. 739-742.

Lawton, Edward J., "Principals and Program Planners Take Notice," National Elementary Principal, Vol. LI (October, 1971), p. 59.

Mills, Patricia, "A Philosophical Base for Curriculum Decisions," Educational Leadership, Vol. 29 (April, 1972), pp. 631-637.

O'Brien, James R., "The Most Important Force for Change," School and Community, Vol. LVIII (April, 1972), p. 44.

Renner, John W., and Thomas W. Wiggins, "The Delusion of Curricular Change: An Alternative," Education, Vol. 91 (April-May, 1971), pp. 319-322.

Rooze, Gene E., "Planning for Curriculum Implementation: A New Perspective," Educational Technology, Vol. XI (July, 1971), pp. 58-60.

PART TWO

Methodology for Conceptual Modification

Chapter 4

IN-SERVICE SYNDROME FOR INSTRUCTIONAL IMPROVEMENT

In-service Education Defined

In-service Education: An Effective Concept. The concept of in-service education is professionally worthy of investing time and finances. At the same time, those responsible for program development have initiated programs, in past decades, which were in need of coordinated management. Therefore, the intended purpose of in-service education is readily accepted as a viable means for faculty-staff improvement. The problem, once again, is misuse of technique. As a result of mismanagement, the in-service concept has fallen into disrepute among many professional educators at all levels of instruction.

Basic Assumptions. When planning for in-service education, supervisory leadership would be more realistic if basic assumptions were not made. Specifically, those in a leadership position cannot allude to preconceptions such as where an individual ought to be and the types of experiences he ought to have had prior to initiating a sequence of in-service education.[1] When preconceptions are made without verification, confusion reigns. Supervisory leadership has been redundant and has created professional confusion due to the fact that the faculty-staff participants did not correctly interpret the intended objectives of the sessions, assuming that they were initially stated. Therefore, pre-in-service orientation of participants becomes a vital factor which

1. Robert Shanon, "A Style for In-service Education," National Elementary Principal, XLVII, No. 4 (February, 1969), p. 24.

determines the success of an in-service program. The quality of faculty-staff participation is a reflection of their own orientation. (Appendix C.)

Contributions of Potential Participants. Even though everyone cannot participate on an "equal" basis, groups of persons who may be participants do have information to contribute. First, a scholar could provide counsel about what is to be taught, identifying concepts and behavioral objectives which concentrate upon the nature of an academic discipline. Second, parents and interested citizens could create channels for sharing professional thinking. The professional faculty has a responsibility for providing this opportunity.[2] Third, a participant seldom consulted in this activity is the student being taught. Pupil-teacher planning could provide valuable insight for problem analysis. Pupils could be involved in determining the following questions in pupil-teacher planning:

1. What is to be studied?
2. Why are we having this learning activity?
3. How shall we go about it?
4. Where do we do what needs to be done?
5. When do we do it?
6. Who will do each part of the job?[3]

Finally, an educator could take data and use it to provide: (1) structure, (2) statesmanship, (3) communication to students with reference to their own values of learning, and (4) inter-relatedness and evaluation of their contributions from many disciplines for the purpose of creating curriculum which will be submitted to a curriculum council or a board of

---

2. Glen Hass, "Who Should Plan the Curriculum?," Educational Leadership, XIX, No. 1 (October, 1961), pp. 3-4, 39.

3. Ibid.

education for approval.[4] As a result, carefully guided interaction of personnel prior to initiating a planned program of in-service education becomes a function of supervisory leadership.

Guidelines for In-service Education Organization

Planning. Once in-service has been accepted as a means for faculty-staff development, there is need to develop an articulated program of supervisory in-service throughout the entire school year. This program has to be in keeping with the school system's: (1) philosophy of education, (2) long-range planning, and (3) the priorities established for the present school year.[5] At preschool workshops, a projected supervisory in-service program should be presented for faculty-staff modification and subsequent approval. Objectives, rationale--for priority selection--, anticipated results and their effect upon curriculum, and instructional improvement should be presented and clarified.

Meeting Frequency. Frequency of faculty-staff in-service meetings should tend not to exceed one school day per month. Many school system administrators have allotted time for such meetings which are approved within state department guidelines. These meetings should be regarded as being important enough to dismiss school activities. Requiring faculty and staff to attend meetings after the close of the work day tends to create negative attitudes toward the supervisory in-service program. From the authors' experience, faculty and staff do not resent participating, but they believe that required attendance is a professional imposition. Required attendance

4. Ibid.

5. Supervisory leadership must function on three levels simultaneously: (1) immediate, (2) short-term, and (3) long-range. Programs should be continuously adjusted and professionally modified for maximum results.

is perceived as an added burden to an already overcrowded work day. Likewise, thoughtful curriculum development has seldom been an attribute of in-service sessions beginning at 4:00 p.m. Task-force groups assigned to specific curriculum development and evaluation should be encouraged and scheduled to meet regularly between the all-district meetings. These small-group sessions coordinated by the supervisory staff should be the basis for involving the larger professional group. Their work serves to expedite the efficient use of time during the in-service sessions.

Meeting Format. The format of the meeting is as important as the success of the orientation and planning sessions. Those responsible for supervisory planning should seek to provide a variety of formats which allow for stimulating continuity. Past observation and participation suggest that there is a propensity to: (1) rely heavily on guest lecturers, (2) overuse resource consultants, (3) divide into aimless committees, and (4) rotate among several seminar groups which tend to become platforms for "axe grinders" or become an "ignorant sharing party" coordinated by a self-anointed believer in "total involvement" under the pretext of being "democratic." Any combination of these becomes a preconceived stereotype by the participants. In time, these sessions may become an activity to "put up with" and avoid whenever possible. Supervisory leadership is reminded that faculty staff desire to be purposefully involved rather than be involved in passive participation where they are talked "at." Format variation, couched within specifically comprehended objectives and anticipated outcomes, allows an individual participant an opportunity to make significant contributions. Planning and meeting format can be separated for the purpose of analysis; however, in reality, these two facets of in-service decision-making are inseparably complementary to each other.

Student-Faculty-Supervisory Role

Student. When surveying need, input from the learner is seldom sought. Regardless of the planned program for him on an immediate, short-term, and long-range basis, the interpretation of it is in terms of now, his real world. Often a student's perspective can assist adult planners to make their proposed plans increasingly relevant. The learner ought to be consistently involved in this planning activity; however, discretion must be exercised so that he is being asked to participate in those areas of concern in which he can make a genuine contribution based upon knowledge. Keep in mind, it has become "fashionable" to provide for student representation, but to include students when working with confidential information and subjects beyond their comprehension is an administrative absurdity.

Teacher. A classroom teacher functions in a dual capacity due to the nature of his position in the involvement scheme. First, he can be an agent for data gathering from learners. Second, he has the responsibility of translating this data and working with his peers and the supervisory staff. (See Figure 4-1.) Faculty contribution is as qualitative as the discretion exercised by the supervisor in seeking information. Parallel to student involvement, teacher participation must be based upon knowledge and work habits. Thus, Mead's concept of lateral transmission[6] is operative at all levels of organizational preparation.

At this level of organizational preparation, the concern is that the instructional faculty keep the educational philosophy and priority selection of the system in focus. Referring to change, the wise use of technology has to be considered.[7] Borrowing Toffler's definition, the student and

---

6. Margaret Mead, "Redefinition of Education," in C. Scott Fisher, ed. Education for Public Responsibility. New York: W. W. Norton & Company, Inc., 1961, p. 57.

7. Alvin Toffler. Future Shock. New York: Bantam Books, 1971, p. 27.

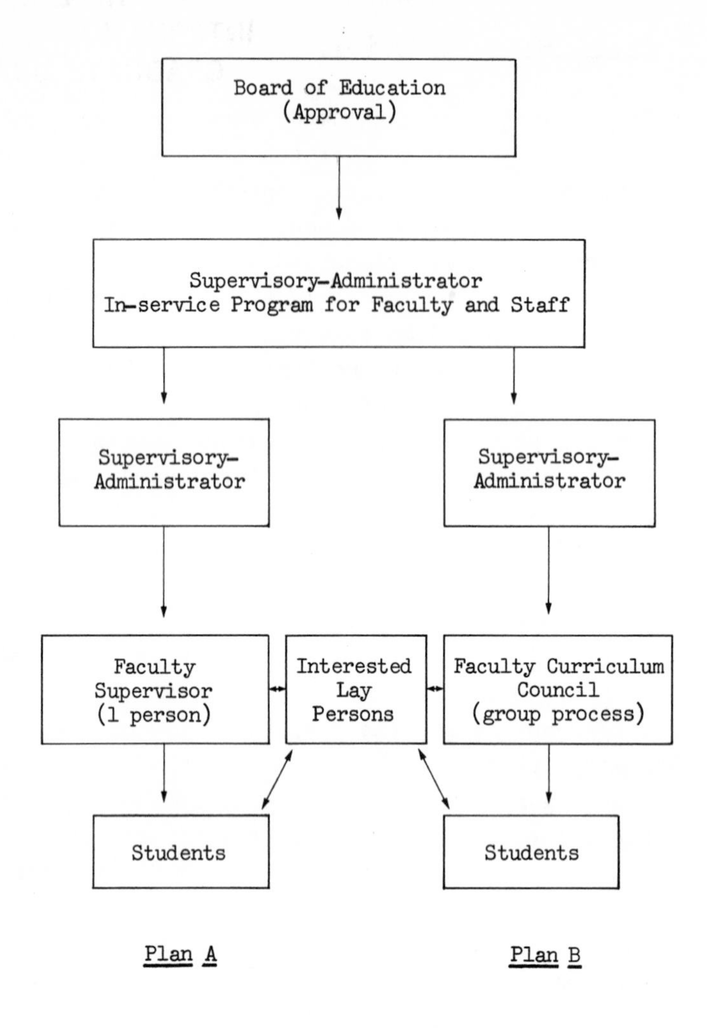

Fig. 4-1

STUDENT-FACULTY AND SUPERVISORY ADMINISTRATOR ROLE IN IN-SERVICE EDUCATION ORGANIZATION

teacher work with creative feasibility and practical application. Accurate decisions at this level of input serve to buttress supervisory potential on an immediate, short-term, and long-range basis. (See Figure 4-1.)

Supervisory-Administrator. Depending upon the size of the school district, Plan A or Plan B would be optional. (See Figure 4-1.) At the level of input, the supervisory-administrative function is one of coordination and diffusion throughout the system.[8] The single purpose of the supervisor-administrator is to facilitate the instructional-learning process for those assigned to classroom instruction. Thus, the final decision for in-service programming organization rests with the administration. Tactful public relations, coupled with observable sincerity in professional behavior, are consistent requirements of this educational leadership. Quality in-service organization will be as operative as the analysis and coordination capability of the supervisor-administrator.

Curriculum Council. The curriculum council in larger districts should in effect be one of recommendation, not policy-making. Composition of this council might include: (1) representatives from grade levels, (2) subject areas, and (3) student representatives. Appointment of students as permanent voting members is not recommended. When feasible, students should be invited to provide information or to undertake work on a specific curriculum assignment. (See Figure 4-1.) Overrepresentation should be avoided.

Special Problems Related to In-service Education

"Ho-hum" Attitude. Due to mediocre and poor quality of in-service programs, faculties throughout the nation have developed a "ho hum" attitude toward in-service as a means for professional improvement. As a result, there is a compelling need by supervisory administration to counteract this dilemma. A "ho-hum" attitude that cannot be changed or re-

---

8. Ibid. "Technological innovation consists of three stages linked into a self-reinforcing cycle. First, there is the creative feasible idea. Second, its practical application. Third, its diffusion through society."

directed undermines the best of in-service planning, regardless of district size.

An Agent of Retreat. In-service education, past and present, serves to impede change and maintain a *status quo* which in effect is a form of retreat. Working to modify and/or extend programs which have proven to be poorly planned and articulated provides glaring insight into supervisory behavior. Perpetuating the *status quo* for the sake of the *status quo* is as unacceptable as change for change's sake. Both positions are unacceptable to the professional planner.

Immaturity of Appointment and Unjustifiable Retention. The best classroom teacher may not have the best supervisory potential. Very often, two situations occur: (1) a supervisor has fulfilled this role for a long period of time and reigns or (2) a neophyte who is a "hot shot" is appointed. The neophyte may be a tool of central administration as opposed to his ability to make a contribution toward the advancement of curriculum development and instructional improvement.

If the concept of lateral transmission is to be consistently implemented, the reassignment of supervisory personnel must be seriously considered. Improvement of the professional quality of a supervisory program depends upon coming to grips with the fact that there comes a time when each of us no longer performs a task commensurate with the professional demands of the time. Especially when a supervisor is responsible for the coordination and implementation of diffused technology in an innovative matrix throughout a given school system, the best of talent is needed. Unless professional integrity rises above tenure and "well-meaningism," the supervisory function is short circuited. This is not to infer that years of service are to be equated with eventual ineffectiveness, because each supervisor must be evaluated on his own individual merits.

A school administrator might consider rotating the supervisory staff in and out of the classroom instruction level so that they do not become isolated in some office bogged down with minutia. Staggering the supervisory staff brings continued relevance into the supervisory program. A supervisory-administrator can easily become concerned with trivia instead of the education of children and young adults.

Superimposition Without Notification. As government funds have been made available to the education sector, many programs have been developed by industry. These programs have merits; however, these programs guided by inexperienced or non-oriented personnel are usually less than successful. Experience shows that many supervisory-administrators have purchased and/or decided upon a new approach to be initiated during the summer recess. A few years ago, modern math was such a victim, and linguistics is receiving the same treatment today. This arbitrary adoption of programs without faculty involvement in the decision function is insuring instructional difficulty because there are teachers who have neither the academic knowledge nor the instructional behavioral competence in the subject areas cited. This precipitous behavior on the part of the supervisory-administrators is characteristic of the so-called avant-garde. Upon closer examination, these arbitrary decisions have often been made without regard to a philosophy of education or priorities based upon long-range planning. A survey of representative schools throughout the nation indicates sporadic involvement--initiation after initiation--where follow-through has not consistently characterized supervision, curriculum development, or in-service education. Analyzing the situation more closely, new programs have been a shoring up of the old with new technology. Old programs and new technology do not produce effective educational experiences. (See Appendix D.)

Statesmanship and Functional In-service Education

Central Concern. In past decades, the demands of society were relatively few, but this is not the case today. To fulfill and maintain the aspirations of a national democracy, the problem of what to teach must be given closer attention.

Herrick suggests that 10 basic questions ultimately must be resolved by those responsible for curriculum development and instructional improvement.

1. What shall determine what is to be taught?
2. How shall we organize and work to decide what is to be taught?
3. What sources shall be used to determine what is to be taught?
4. Shall we provide a comprehensive curriculum for all children and youth?
5. What shall we regard as general and specialized education?
6. How shall we maintain a balance in what is taught?
7. What subject areas deserve immediate consideration?
8. How shall we teach what is to be taught?
9. How shall we finance what is to be taught?
10. How shall we evaluate the subjects that are taught?[9]

Area in Need of Statesmanship. Diplomacy and astute statesmanship are as much a part of successful educational ventures as they are of international politics. The coordination of those activities which bring about a purposeful resolution of the 10 issues in question requires no less than diplomatic brilliance. The continual analysis of such an assignment is central to effective statesmanship. Of the issues posed by Herrick, the authors consider one to be basic and fundamental to the resolution of the rest. Determining what resources will be utilized in deciding what is to be taught clearly demonstrates to the professional and tax-

---

9. Theral T. Herrick, "Curriculum Problems: Some Basic Issues," Teacher College Record, LX, No. 5 (February, 1959), pp. 242-244.

paying community the educational philosophy, or lack of one, that serves to guide any given school system. Tyler suggests that determination of curriculum might come from such defensible sources as: (1) study of the learner, (2) contemporary life, (3) subject matter specialists, (4) philosophy, and (5) the psychology of learning.[10]

Any one source which dominates another skews the decision; however, if it is a priority of intent, then such a decision would be acceptable. But to provide substance to statesmanship, the following statements should be a guide in making a decision: (1) it is important to know how a particular group of students learn so that the selected programs are relevant to their style of learning versus the learner's adjusting to the instructional style of the classroom teacher, (2) philosophy will guide selectivity with reference to priority selection, (3) contemporary living provides perspective, and (4) the subject-matter specialist has the capacity to suggest the specifics of the cognitive domain to forge out priorities and desired behavioral objectives.

Supervisory statesmanship requires loyalty to a basic philosophy and established priorities coupled with a capacity to bring about desired changes and retain professional continuity without infringing upon teacher style. Commitment, discipline, and adaptability are the three characteristics required for successful statesmanship. In fact, supervisory-administrative statesmanship is one of those professional roles seldom sought; however, effective statesmanship can make all the difference.

Summary

In-service education is an effective means to improve curriculum development, faculty/staff leadership, and in-

---

10. Ralph W. Tyler. Basic Principles of Curriculum and Instruction Syllabus for Education 360. Chicago: The University of Chicago Press, 1950, pp. 4-28.

structional competence. However, supervisory leadership should refrain from making basic assumptions concerning knowledge and competence levels of performance prior to program initiation. To assist in upgrading relevance of in-service programs, counselling with appropriate persons who have worthwhile contributions to make is encouraged.

Successful in-service education depends primarily upon the quality of planning, meeting frequency, and variety of format. Special problems that plague in-service education need to be diminished or eliminated. These include: (1) negative attitude toward in-service management, (2) an attempt to use in-service as a means for maintaining the status quo, (3) immature supervisory appointment, (4) unjustifiable retention of ineffective personnel, and (5) the foisting of programs upon the faculty and staff without previous professional preparation to carry them out.

Effective supervisory-administrative personnel are required to coordinate divergent assortments of hidden agendas and weld them into a purposeful program in consonance with a school system's educational philosophy and long-range planning. To accomplish this task, supervisory-administrative leadership has to: (1) be loyal to a philosophy of education, (2) believe in the designated priorities which should provide for professional continuity, and (3) safeguard the integrity of an individual classroom teacher's instructional style and his right to improve his leadership potential.

Major Themes

1. In-service education as a means to improve faculty-staff competence is considered a worthy undertaking but often suffers from professional mismanagement.
2. Supervisory-administrative personnel should refrain from making assumptions concerning levels of competence prior to initiation of an in-service program.
3. Students, faculty, and interested lay persons, all potential participants, should have an opportunity

to make a contribution prior to in-service program decision.

4. In-service education should be developed in terms of immediate, short-term, and long-range planning.
5. The ongoing in-service program should reflect the educational philosophy, priority designation, and long-range planning of the school district.
6. Meeting frequency should be purposefully planned to include all-district and task-force work sessions.
7. The format of in-service sessions should vary so as to promote and sustain faculty-staff participation.
8. Student, faculty, and supervisory-administrators have specific roles to fulfill in the process of in-service organization.
9. For large districts, a curriculum council may serve as an agent to facilitate supervisory management.
10. A "ho-hum" attitude, misuse of in-service sessions to maintain a <u>status quo</u>, immaturity of appointment, unjustifiable retention of personnel, and the superimposition of programming without notification are basic problems which serve to undermine the effectiveness of an in-service program.
11. Demands of society require more qualified supervisory personnel who can accurately analyze complex issues which need resolution in order to perpetuate the national democracy.
12. The determination of what sources will be used to select what is to be taught is the focal point of supervisory-administrative decision-making, which in turn affects the resolution of all other educational issues.
13. Statesmanship is required of supervisory-administrative leadership in order to create and sustain a viable in-service program.

Enrichment Readings

Bishop, Leslee J., "In-service Education: Balance and Thrust," Educational Leadership, Vol. 25 (October, 1967), pp. 10-11.

Snyder, Fred, "Supervisory Roles of Elementary Principals," Contemporary Education, Vol. XXXIX (May, 1968), pp. 274-275.

Supplementary Readings

Allen, Dwight W., and Glenn W. Hawkes, "Reconstruction of Teacher Education and Professional Growth Program or How the Third Little Pig Escaped the Wolf," Phi Delta Kappan, Vol. 52 (September, 1970), pp. 4-13.

Bruell, Edwin, "The Supervisor Supervises Himself," Education Vol. 89 (September-October), pp. 74-77.

Chesin, Gerald A., "Group Dynamics and In-service Education," Peabody Journal of Education, Vol. 44 (May, 1967), pp. 350-352.

Felker, Donald W., Jacob Goering, and Kathryn W. Linden, "Teacher Rigidity and Continuing Education," Journal of Teacher Education, Vol. 22 (Winter, 1971), pp. 460-463.

Foreman, Milton E., William A. Poppen, and Jack M. Frost, "Case Groups: An In-service Education Technique," The Personnel and Guidance Journal, Vol. 46 (December, 1967), pp. 388-392.

Foster, Walter S., "Teachers' Opinions: Their Implications for In-service Education," National Elementary Principal, Vol. XLV (April, 1966), pp. 48-51.

Ingils, C. R., "Group Dynamics--Boon or Bane?" The Personnel and Guidance Journal, Vol. 46 (April, 1968), pp. 744-748.

Thomas, David, "T-Grouping: The White-Collar Hippie Movement," Phi Delta Kappan, Vol. XLIX (April, 1968), pp. 458-460.

Wooton, Lutian R., "The Professional Teacher Keeps Pace," The Peabody Journal of Education, Vol. 43 (March, 1966), pp. 299-301.

Chapter 5

OBSERVATION FOR INSTRUCTIONAL IMPROVEMENT

Determining the Focus of Assistance. Delineating an area for assistance becomes a primary activity for supervisory leadership. Focus of assistance then becomes a function of educational philosophy and priority designation. Without priority designation there can be no focus of intent. Aligned with educational philosophy and priority designation are the concerns: (1) Who will be involved? (2) What assistance is needed? (3) What rate of phase-in is realistic? Very often supervisory leadership is accused of data gathering without analysis and implementation, not unlike the guidance counselor. Kopp and McNeff originally developed their model for elementary school guidance; however, the principle is adaptable in determining the focus of assistance.[1] (Figure 5-1.)

Discussion with grass-roots teachers throughout the nation indicates a continuum of input, initiation of projects, and limited follow-through. No sooner has one project been initiated than another is being prepared, which results in curriculum development and instruction being at cross variance, or one of joining the ranks of being experimentally fashionable. Experimentation should be encouraged; however, purposeful programming must be coordinated and followed through to its termination by an evaluation of the predetermined terminal objectives. When overinitiation characterizes a school system, focus of assistance has not been sys-

1. O. W. Kopp and Marie E. McNeff. Guidance Handbook for Personnel of Elementary Schools. Lincoln, Nebraska: The University of Nebraska Press, 1969.

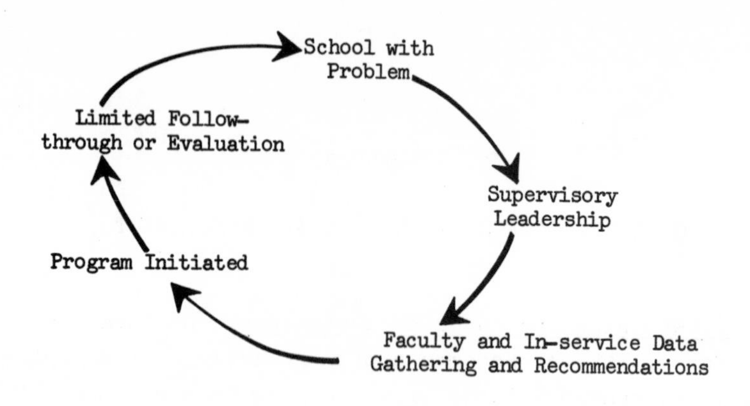

Fig. 5-1

ENDLESS CIRCLE OF INPUT--INITIATION
AND LIMITED FOLLOW-THROUGH

tematically determined, and the worthwhileness of professional activity becomes questionable.

In contrast, purposeful focus of assistance can be identified and made operative. (Figure 5-2.) Focus of assistance can be determined and implemented when projects are: (1) phased-in, (2) subject to modification, (3) followed up, and (4) subjected to objective evaluation.[2]

2. Evaluation instruments should be designed and/or selected prior to project initiation. There have been instances noted by the authors where: (1) standardized tests were selected which were not in keeping with the stated objectives, hence, inaccurate results were recorded; (2) a testing tool was selected or designed to present the findings in a better frame of reference than actually was the case. In both instances, an act of unscrupulous educational practice serves to undermine public confidence. This cannot be permitted by responsible supervisory leadership.

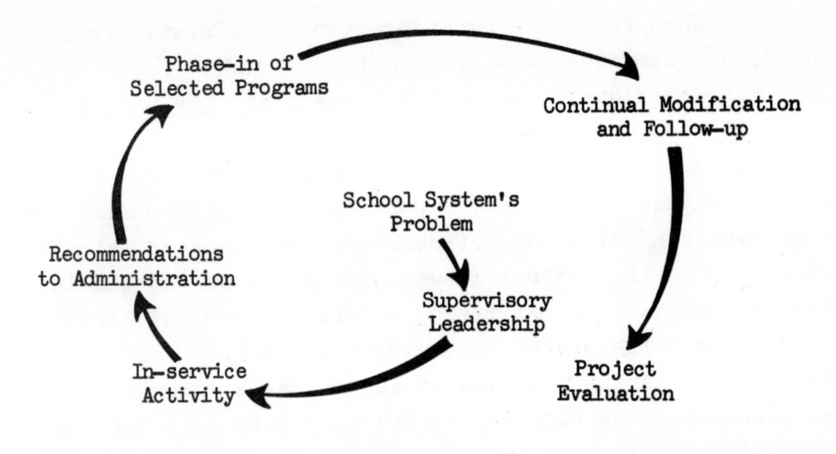

Fig. 5-2

IDENTIFICATION OF FOCUS AND MEANINGFUL IMPLEMENTATION

Assessment of Drift from Established Objectives. Although instructional style makes for pupil interest and variety in the learning process, there is a dual responsibility of supervisory leadership and classroom teacher to provide those experiences which are in keeping with program objectives. Teacher style should not be confused with academic license. Academic license is an arrogance that cannot be tolerated in an established set of experiences designed for established terminal criterion performance objectives.

Teaching style, a personal catalyst, is developed by those who work at the art of educating. Yet, style should not be allowed to overshadow the relevance of content for assimilation. Drift from established objectives is continually being determined by supervisory leadership. Such drift can be detected by observing: (1) the quality and kind of participation by a teacher during in-service sessions and (2) the variance from normative performance of children in attendance. A conference with personnel with reference to associated activities should assist students in applying acquired knowledge. Drift from established objectives is a subtle phenomena. When there are no objectives, on a system-wide basis, all learning is adrift continually.

Evaluate Instructional Environment and the Utilization of Facilities. Evaluation of instructional utilization of facilities at this point must deal with attitudes. Before an evaluation can be enacted, supervisory leadership must create a climate conducive to professional introspection which focuses upon the central issues of whether or not the instructional team is maximizing effort in terms of terminal objectives. Therefore, supervisory leadership has the challenge of assisting the faculty as well as the community in comprehending the existing effort in relation to what might be realistically developed to educate youth. An attitude must be realized which allows the educational team to take a "look" for what it "is." When this condition exists, a more realistic evaluation may be obtained.

Before the initiation of the instruction, facilities should be ascertained. Because of a lack of appraisal prior to change requests, many worthy programs have been and will continue to be voted down, let alone be given a fair hearing. Some criteria for evaluation of worthiness of programs are: (1) teacher centeredness versus pupil centeredness, (2) lecture versus problem-solving techniques, (3) textbook-workbook versus instructional material center orientation, (4) prescriptive instruction by design versus chapter by chapter based, (5) taxonomy level of instruction, a continuum of knowledge and comprehension, versus application and invention, (6) accentuation of the whole class versus small group and personalized instruction, (7) team teaching versus team planning and irrelevant instruction, and (8) appropriate integration of audio-visual aids versus omission of any whatsoever. Thus, guidelines should be established relative to the evaluation of instructional environment and faculty use. Without accurate data, the request for support is questionable. Daraio reminds the supervising principal that his instructional leadership is assured when the faculty and community perceive him as being sincere and willing to work with them. Then a supervisory principal has an opportunity to lead into new directions.[3]

<u>Elements of the Observation Visit</u>. Observation in the classroom is fundamental to the supervisory process. "Of the various techniques used by principals for supervising the program, none exceeds in effectiveness or in helpfulness than that of constructively purposeful visitations. Consistent and continuous contact with teachers focused upon the instructional program seems to be a basis to effective supervision."[4] Planning is primary to the observation technique. Curtin states that if planning were conscientiously followed, two improvements would immediately arise: "(1) there would be a sharp reduction in the number of aimless and whimsical classroom observations and (2) the classroom observations that were carried would tend to be far more pointed and directed."[5] The supervisor can undertake activities which can insure potential success. These include: (1) planning with a teacher, (2) reviewing the records of previous visits, (3) perusing records of the class's performance before the visit, and (4) consulting the file of appropriate and previous supervisory conferences.[6] In addition, Curtin suggests three useful generalizations that can be applied to various situations: (1) establish a purpose for the observation, (2) outline procedures and materials to be used, and (3) make provision for evaluation of the observation.[7]

---

3. Peter J. Daraio, "Principal Role Leading Staff with New Attitudes," <u>Instructor</u>, LXXXI, No. 5 (January, 1972), p. 31. Reprinted from <u>Instructor</u>, © January, 1972, The Instructor Publications, Inc. Used by permission.

4. Department of Elementary School Principals, NEA. "The Elementary School Principalship: A Research Study, 37th Yearbook." Washington, D.C.: <u>National Elementary Principal</u>, 1958, p. 34.

5. James Curtin. <u>Supervision in Today's Elementary Schools</u>. New York: The Macmillan Company, 1964, p. 67.

6. <u>Ibid</u>., p. 68.

7. <u>Ibid</u>., p. 69.

The previously listed generalizations are not consistently practiced. Regretfully, many a supervisory observation remains a "chitchat" or an unannounced visit where the classroom teacher is unaware of the pending visit. Hence, the classroom teacher is vulnerable to criticism, which may be unwarranted. The supervisory observation is one which should assist in the long-range improvement of teacher instruction and subsequent curriculum improvement for the learner. The purpose of the observation visitation is to "help" not to "indiscriminately criticize." The observation visitation is a time for analysis, during which the supervisory assistance provided helps the instructional faculty to help themselves. Thus, purposeful planning becomes a primary activity of every supervisor as he carries out his program.

Behavioral Guidelines for Classroom Observation. Assuming the observation has been planned by the supervisor with the classroom teacher, focus must be placed upon the role of the supervisor as an observer. The supervisor has one function--to analyze the instructional setting--for the purpose of instructional improvement. Without an articulated program, the supervisor cannot analyze in terms of specific details which lend themselves to long-range curriculum objectives. Thus, analysis of follow-up conferences can have import only within the context of a defined program of supervision.

The inherent danger is one of confusing a planned observation visitation with a casual visit. Those supervisors who state that they are in the classroom continually usually observe very little because their reasons for observing are not clear. While they have a set of general impressions, which may report a status of instructional level, the supervisors more often than not have no developed plan of instructional improvement. Specific recommendations for classroom supervisory behavior include:

1. Requesting the classroom teacher to notify pupils of the forthcoming visit and something about the reason for the visit.

2. Remaining in one place in the classroom and entering the activities when invited, trying not to disrupt the ongoing work.

3. Preparing a check list in advance relative to the focus of the visit so that a minimum of note taking will be done.

4. If video tape or tape recorders are being used, making sure the decision for their use is a part of the initial planning session. The equipment should be set up in advance of the supervisor's arrival.

5. Making arrangements for a follow-up conference before leaving the school building.

Since a supervisor is concerned with effective utilization of teaching tools, he should be seeking information concerning the following questions as he observes any instructional setting:

1. Are pupils using reference materials other than the basic text?

2. How effectively are workbooks being employed?

3. To what extent and how effectively is programmed learning being used?

4. Are audio-visual materials being utilized to the greatest advantage?

5. What is the quality and quantity of homework that is being assigned?[8]

The answers to these and other questions can be acquired only through the observation technique. A variety of observation plans are acceptable; however, Neagley and Evans suggest three types of observation to provide a supervisor with an overview of the educational program at the instructional level. First, he should visit a classroom before the chil-

---

8. Ross L. Neagley and N. Dean Evans. Handbook for Effective Supervision of Instruction. Englewood Cliffs, N.J.: Prentice-Hall Inc., 1964, p. 131.

dren arrive, or later in the afternoon when school has been dismissed for the day. Second, he should make visits in a series. Short visits to a large number of classrooms bring the general-learning climate into sharp focus. Third, he should plan to visit and participate in the activities in progress.[9]

As a change agent, a supervisor must always be aware of the fact that his interpreted behavior can serve to advance or impede quality learning for youth. Since observation is basic to supervision, Crosby brings the act of supervision into perspective when she writes:

> Observation throws new light upon the quality of learning experiences in a teaching situation. The kind of experiences provided, the relationship between and among the various experiences, the roles of the teacher and children in planning and evaluating their experiences, and the quality of planning revealed are factors which must be analyzed when teacher and supervisor work together to help the teacher provide for more effective curriculum building with children.[10]

In keeping with the planned visitation, a follow-up conference should be arranged by the supervisor with the classroom teacher. Since teachers perceive the supervisory visit as a signficant event, the conference and memorandum statement should be carefully planned. Consistency is required for both the conference and the recorded data in the memorandum. Therefore, the following guidelines can assist a supervisor in preparing for both the follow-up conference and the written memorandum:

1. Begin with a positive statement.
2. Avoid mention of any information about which there is doubt.

---

9. Ibid., pp. 132-133.

10. Muriel Crosby. Supervision as Co-operative Action. New York: Appleton-Century-Crofts, 1957, p. 52. Reprinted by permission of Prentice-Hall, Inc., Englewood Cliffs, New Jersey.

3. Criticism should always be tentative with suggestions for improvement or modification.

4. The tone of the communication whether in conference or written communication is as important as its content.[11] (Appendix E.)

The practice of statesmanship both in the conference and in the written memorandum is equally important to the success of any supervisory program. In the final analysis, the supervisory personality is a key factor in both initiating and successfully sustaining effective observation and follow-up exercises. As a result, increased quality learning for youth can be the outcome of the supervisor's efforts.

<u>Summary</u>

Observation for instructional improvement is the primary technique implemented by the supervisor. Its impact is apparent when the observing supervisor works within the framework of a planned instructional program. As a result, the determination of focus for the supervisory visitation becomes a continual activity of every supervisor. Focus can be determined only when projects are phased-in, subject to modification, follow-up, and subjected to objective evaluation. The observation technique is used to ascertain the drift from established objectives. Here a supervisor is concerned with teacher style, academic license, and the experiences which lead toward the attainment of predetermined criterion performance objectives. In addition, the observation technique is utilized to determine the quality of instructional environment and the utilization of facilities.

Planning is primary to the professional use of the observation technique. Without careful planning, the visitation becomes aimless and whimsical in character. Thus, educational statesmanship becomes the first order of supervisory

---

11. Curtin, <u>op</u>. <u>cit</u>., pp. 76-76.

behavior. Not to be overlooked is the follow-up conference. Due to the nature of the conference and written memorandum, a supervisor must exercise objective consistency. In the final analysis, supervisory personality becomes the key factor in initiating and sustaining effective observation and follow-up experiences.

Major Themes

1. Observation visitations assist in determining the focus of assistance which is a primary activity of supervisory leadership and reflects its educational philosophy and priority designation.
2. For many school faculty members, there is participation in an endless circle of input and initiation with limited follow-through.
3. Purposeful focus can be implemented when projects are phased in, subject to modification, followed up, and subjected to objective evaluation.
4. Evaluation instruments should be designed and/or selected in consonance with determined objectives prior to project initiation.
5. Observation visitations assist in assessing the drift from established objectives.
6. Observation visitations are used to evaluate instructional environment and the faculty's utilization of facilities to attain instructional objectives.
7. Planning is primary to the successful use of the observation technique by a supervisor.
8. The purpose of an observation visitation is to "help" not to "indiscriminately criticize."
9. The supervisor's behavior while in the classroom and his interrelationships with the classroom teacher and children are fundamental to the success of the observation visit.

10. Each supervisor must select an appropriate mix of visitation types which will provide accurate information desired for analysis.
11. The follow-up conference and memorandum should exhibit consistency.
12. The tone of communication during the follow-up conference and the language used in the memorandum are as important as the content.
13. In the final analysis, the supervisory personality is a key factor in both initiating and sustaining effective observation and follow-up experiences with any given faculty.

Enrichment Readings

Amidon, Edmund J., Kathleen M. Kies, and Anthony T. Palisi, "Group Supervision: A Technique for Improving Teaching Behavior," National Elementary Principal, Vol. XLV (April, 1966), pp. 54-58.

Lucas, Carmen W., "Is It Really Necessary for Principals to Visit Classrooms?," Elementary School Journal, Vol. 66 (February, 1966), pp. 245-248.

Supplementary Readings

Blumberg, Arthur, and Philip Cusick, "Supervisor-Teacher Interaction: An Analysis of Verbal Behavior," Education, Vol. 91 (November, 1970), pp. 126-134.

Brown, Bob Burton, "Observer-Judge Ratings of Teacher Competence," Childhood Education, Vol. 44 (November, 1967), pp. 205-207.

Hungerford, John I., "Should a Teacher Be Exempt from Supervisory Visits?," Instructor, Vol. 78 (January, 1969), p. 37.

Hunter, Madeline, "When the Supervisor Innovates," Instructor, Vol. 77 (March, 1968), p. 31.

Meredith, Richard A., "Supervision Has Been a Destructive Force in Education," Ohio Schools, Vol. 46 (September, 1968), pp. 19-20.

Neil, Herschel L., "The Case for Classroom Visitation," School and Community, Vol. 53 (May, 1967), p. 44.

Null, Elden J., "The Hierarchy of Personal Needs: Its Significance to School Principals," Peabody Journal of Education, Vol. 47 (May, 1970), pp. 347-351.

Tout, Dr. John R., "Solving Problems Together," School and Community, Vol. 55 (October, 1968), p. 16.

Chapter 6

CONFERENCES AND STAFF MEETINGS FOR INSTRUCTIONAL IMPROVEMENT

Purpose Defined. The supervisory conference and staff meeting should provide an opportunity for the classroom teacher and supervisor to discuss specific aspects of the educational enterprise. This definition suggests that both the conference and staff meeting should be specific and should focus upon an aspect of curriculum. Within this context, Curtin lists seven purposes for which a conference could serve the central focus of supervision: (1) work toward self-directed improvement, (2) capitalize on strengths, (3) aid in analysis of the learning situation, (4) administer criticisms, (5) plan for classroom observations, (6) evaluate instructional procedure, and (7) set goals for instructional improvement.[1] A defined purpose for a conference is fundamental to the success of anticipated outcomes. This is also true for staff meetings. The lack of comprehended purpose by the participants serves as an agent for establishing internal resistance to supervisory/administrative efforts.

Agent for Instructional Problem Identification. Instructional problems can be identified more readily in a conference setting than in a large group meeting. An instructional problem can be determined best in the conference setting because the dialogue is more personal and usually without argument. Naive supervisory/administrative personnel often initiate discussion in the large staff meeting only to create supervisory problems for themselves. Obtaining a consensus

---

1. James Curtin. Supervision in Today's Elementary Schools. New York: The Macmillan Company, 1964, p. 94.

prior to the initiation of discussion provides supervisory leadership with a firm basis for operation because his problem identification list will represent faculty judgment. Consensus by conference brings the supervisory personality into focus on a personal basis. The one-to-one contact prior to the larger staff in-service meeting characterizes effective public relations. Thus, when problems are selected for analysis in a staff meeting, the general faculty will have had direct involvement in decision-making.

Formulation of Ways to Solve Identified Problems. Formulating ways to solve identified problems is a complex process. (Appendix F.) Unlike many functions, ways of arriving at solutions are more readily determined by supervisory leadership characterized by flexibility. Conversely, rigidity in supervisory leadership serves to thwart many able, flexible faculty to the point that they seek other employment or give "lip service" in order to appear cooperative. When flexibility guides the formulation of determining ways to solve instructional problems, there is a better chance that the solution will be long-range oriented rather than a stop-gap measure.

A supervisor can aid in the determination of ways to solve identified problems by genuinely taking the faculty into his confidence and eliciting their suggestions for ways that could be realistically implemented. This is not to be interpreted as having the faculty do the supervisor's work, because his primary function is to motivate. By assisting the staff to help themselves, the supervisor is building self-confidence in the instructional faculty. Within the conference setting, a tactful and experienced supervisor assists in bringing perspective to an isolated problem. Again, by using a consensus approach, a supervisor can bring unanimity to the problem-solving task.

The supervisor who works with his staff in formulating ways to solve identified problems will create meaningful approaches to problem-solving because he will have implemented supervisory guidance function which employs the expertise of the faculty. Here the supervisory role is one of coordinating the participants' input so as to bring about the best possible solution and alternatives in terms of both the instructional staff and the learner.

<u>Emphasis Placed on Self-directed Improvement</u>. Self-directed improvement is the only approach to supervision which insures carry-over into the actual instruction setting. Most personnel desire assistance; however, over the years, some seem to have lost that desire. Through the conference technique, a supervisor can assume the role of an emotionally detached second party who can observe from the sidelines. By assuming this role, a supervisor can assist another teacher to be more objective about his instructional skills and abilities.

Self-improvement is based upon self-confidence. Therefore, a supervisory-classroom teacher conference cannot become a series of critical statements which serve to undermine another person. The supervisory conference should be motivationally oriented with an emphasis upon the work that has been undertaken in a positive manner, and then should describe ways and means by which the classroom teacher could improve where skills and abilities show some limitations. Supervisory commentary should refrain from dwelling upon such topics as "dedication," and "good teaching." This approach tends to be interpreted by the classroom teacher as a session dominated by platitudes and pompous behavior by the supervisor. Thus, the supervisor has damaged his supervisor-teacher relations.

<u>Planning for Conferences and Faculty Meetings</u>. Because time is of the essence, meetings should be carefully designed so that they are interpreted as worthwhile by the participants. Thus, the supervisory conference must be thoroughly planned in advance of the meeting. Too often, the conference has a tendency to be both irrelevant and critical. A supervisory conference should accent and capitalize on strengths; however, it affords an opportunity to be a means to analyze the learning situation. At this time, plans for future instruction can be discussed. Curtin provides a supervisor with a list of salient questions which assist in the analysis of the instructional setting. They are:

1. What were the behavioral objectives for the work?
2. Did the objectives take into account the variation of learning abilities and rates of learning of the pupils?
3. Did the children comprehend the objectives of prescribed instructional formats as stated or written by the teacher?
4. Were the instructional materials varied so that all of the children could achieve success with one or more of the selected media?
5. Did the learning experiences emphasize discovery and problem-solving where the student was an active learner rather than a recipient of cognitive knowledge?
6. Did the learning experiences proceed from the known to the unknown in a sequence which lead from concrete references to increasingly more abstract thinking?
7. Were the evaluative tools and techniques consistent with the behavioral objectives in testing the intended outcome?
8. Did the results from the evaluation techniques provide significant data with which to modify teaching strategies?
9. Did item analysis of evaluation data reveal what was needed to be retaught as well as to whom?

This list of questions should be viewed as a means of assisting the classroom teacher to self-critique his work and not to illustrate what a supervisor considers to be correct or not correct. These questions serve as guidelines for instructional improvement.

When planning for a supervisory conference, the following should be clarified with the classroom teacher: (1) a review of the purpose of the intended conference, (2) a mutual decision as to what will be covered within the conference, and (3) an agreement as to the time, place, and length of the conference. An astute supervisor realizes that a lengthy conference accomplishes little and often antagonizes both of the conference participants. The following guidelines are suggested for carrying out an effective supervisory conference.

1. Begin the conference with positive comments.
2. Be tactful, do not begin with serious matters immediately. Make the classroom teacher feel at ease. It is much easier for you to adjust under the circumstances than the classroom teacher.
3. In the beginning of the conference, concentrate upon those items which have produced observable success.
4. Should there be a discussion about matters that call for improvement, be sure that the classroom teacher understands the problem and realizes a need for assistance. The classroom teacher should also know how your suggested assistance will be of direct benefit to his professional improvement.
5. Be careful; do not attempt to accomplish an unreasonable amount of material in one conference setting. You must be astutely sensitive to timing and conference fatigue on the part of the teacher participant. You should work from the point of clarification and cooperation rather than quantity coverage and administrative efficiency.

Every teacher will leave the supervisory conference with attitudes toward the supervisor, himself, and his functional role as an educator in a particular school system. Thus, the supervisor is the primary force in building professional self-concept. Self-concept becomes the basis upon which quality education can be obtained.

In retrospect, many a zealous supervisor, insensitive to tempo and timing, has pressed on in terms of administrative efficiency only to create public relations problems for himself, which in turn spread throughout the school system. In order to prevent this situation from happening, tactfulness is stressed because a supervisor must set and maintain the professional tone of the supervisory conference.

Similarly, the planning for the staff meetings with reference to in-service must exhibit characteristics which dispel the "ho-hum" attitude. These sessions should be a series of preplanned meetings where each faculty member is informed about topics to be discussed and projects to be worked upon during the school year. In addition, the faculty should know the specific objectives to be accomplished at each meeting. An advance distribution of an agenda which lists the objectives to be achieved and specific follow-up data to the faculty is necessary. From the analysis of each staff meeting, follow-up and transitional activities can be developed prior to the next staff meeting. The integrity of the staff meeting can be recaptured by pointing out to the faculty the successful effects of their contributions and complimenting them for their efforts.

Summary

The supervisory conference and staff meeting should provide a means whereby specific problems of the educational enterprise can be discussed. For effective supervision, the purpose of conferences and staff meetings should be defined. Acquiring a consensus throughout individual conferences provides information for instructional identification. Implementation of the supervisory guidance function greatly assists in a flexible solution of instructional problems because faculty expertise is coordinated to maximize professional efforts in problem-solving.

Self-directed improvement is emphasized because self-concept is increased, which carries over to a more realistic analysis of the instructional setting. Conferences and staff meetings should be preplanned, and specific objectives and intended outcomes should be understood by the participants. Faculties that are continually informed by supervisory leadership which emphasizes the impact of faculty effort upon observable change assist in regaining the integrity of both the supervisory conference and the staff meeting as a means for instructional improvement.

Major Themes

1. Supervisory conference and staff meetings should provide an opportunity for the discussion of specific aspects of the educational enterprise.
2. A defined purpose is fundamental to the success of anticipated outcomes.
3. The supervisory conference can be utilized successfully to determine instructional problem identification.
4. Obtaining a consensus prior to a supervisory staff meeting insures effective in-service programs.
5. Solving identified problems is a complex process.
6. Supervisory leadership characterized by flexibility or rigidity affects problem-solving potential.
7. Supervisory guidance function is a coordination of input at conferences and staff meetings for the purpose of obtaining appropriate solutions for identified instructional problems.
8. Self-directed improvement is an approach to supervision which insures carry-over into the instructional setting.
9. Self-improvement is based upon self-confidence.
10. Planning for conferences and faculty-staff meetings is essential for success.
11. The supervisory conference should capitalize upon the instructional strengths of the observed classroom teacher.
12. The supervisory conference and staff meeting should be positive in orientation with planned follow-up communication.
13. Consistent reporting to the faculty, and showing where their efforts have influenced change, contributes to reestablishing integrity to the super-

visory conference and staff meetings as a means for instructional improvement.

Enrichment Readings

Crispin, David B., and Duane Peterson, "An Analysis of Interaction Among Principals and Teachers During School Faculty Meetings," Contemporary Education, Vol. 39 (May, 1968), pp. 287-290.

Jordan, William C., "'Osmosis'--The New Supervision," Educational Leadership, Vol. 25 (October, 1967), pp. 54-61.

Saville, Anthony, "Breathe New Life into Faculty Meetings," Clearing House, Vol. 39 (September, 1964), pp. 40-42.

Supplementary Readings

Brown, Alan F., and Barry D. Anderson, "Faculty Consensus as a Function of Leadership Frequency and Style," The Journal of Experimental Education, Vol. 36 (Winter, 1967), pp. 43-49.

Delahanty, Brother David, F.S.C., "Communicating with Your Staff," Catholic School Journal, Vol. 38 (March, 1968), pp. 47-48.

Erickson, James R., "How to Kill a Good Principal," Clearing House, Vol. 41 (April, 1967), pp. 483-486.

Henderson, Charles A., "The Principal Speaks," Childhood Education, Vol. 42 (March, 1966), pp. 411-413.

Logan, Sister Fidelis, M.S., "The Principal as Communicator," Catholic School Journal, Vol. 67 (September, 1967), pp. 64-67.

McGrew, John F., "Improving Staff Communications," Clearing House, Vol. 40 (April, 1966), pp. 475-477.

White, Warren, "No Hiding Place," Peabody Journal of Education (May, 1964), pp. 350-353.

PART THREE

Accountability for Instructional Improvement

Chapter 7

EVALUATION OF TEACHING

Problems of Teacher Evaluation. When attempting to evaluate teachers, the concept of evaluation must be considered. Feyereisen et al. define supervison as a systematic process for judging the adequacy of the achievement of the objectives within the school system.[1] If this premise is acceptable, then the supervisor should examine his definition of evaluation. Usually, evaluation implies measurement; however, evaluation is a more inclusive concept and embraces the total of instruction in contrast to accenting one or more parts of the educational enterprise. Teacher evaluation is a serious activity and it should be high on the list of priority assignments for supervisory attention.

In order to evaluate teachers, the supervisor should have a set of conditions created which would allow him to effectively perform this task. These conditions are: (1) a cooperative working relationship between classroom teachers and local attendance unit administrators, (2) the recaptured integrity of the supervisory conference and staff meetings which would allow faculty members to know that stated objectives are being accomplished, (3) supervision which is thought of as being an agent for constructive assistance, (4) accessibility to data, and (5) sufficient time to carry out this aspect of his assignment in a professional manner.

Even though the conditions are conducive to teacher evaluation, there are problems which may prevent a supervisor

---

1. Kathryn V. Feyereisen, A. John Fiorino, and Arlene T. Nowak. Supervision and Curriculum Renewal: A Systems Approach. New York: Appleton-Century-Crofts, 1970, p. 302. Reprinted by permission of Prentice-Hall, Inc., Englewood Cliffs, New Jersey.

from performing this assigned task at the desired level of professional competence. These dysfunctions include: (1) an excessive supervisory load, (2) a severity of problems which need to be solved and which need more attention than time permits, (3) the incidence of problems to be solved that are not only overwhelming but of such character as to be spread throughout the entire school system, (4) a supervisory staff which lack supportive assistance and serve to thwart achievement of stated objectives, (5) a low teacher-administrative morale, and (6) an uncomprehended relationship of supervision to instructional improvement. Not unlike the classroom teacher, a supervisor-administrator may be faced with dysfunctions which coalesce to diminish the quality of teacher evaluation.

Teacher evaluations can be effective and rise above a myriad of dysfunctions which serve to restrict this activity when the process is: (1) specific, (2) comprehensive, (3) based upon documented evidence, (4) inclusive of preplanned conferences, and (5) supplemented with follow-up activity. Thus, effective teacher evaluation is affected by the interrelatedness of each component in consonance with stated educational objectives. (Appendix G.)

Total Evaluation a Continuous Process. As a continuous process, total evaluation must come to grips with work evaluation which implies that there are some supervisors who predict and some who systematically observe a teacher's performance. The predictor seldom observes the instructional setting and runs the risk of making erroneous conclusions. The predictor is more characteristic of one who has a measurement attitude in contrast to a supervisor with an evaluation attitude. The attitude exhibited by a supervisor influences both his behavior and his analysis in the evaluation process.

Combining the supervisory guidance function with cybernetic systems analysis, in consonance with problem-solving and feedback, generates continuous personalized evaluation. Essential to an evaluation program for teacher evaluation is that it should include: (1) clearly stated objectives, (2) a regular and systematic program of activity, (3) an integrated continuously-planned program of activity, (4) an information-storage- and -retrieval system, and (5) the continuous in-service education of the staff.[2]

In this context, in-service education must include the personalized supervisory conference. Through an appropriate selection of activity, teacher evaluation becomes a continuous and personalized sequence of activity.

Administrative Behavior. Within the context of teacher evaluation, administrative behavior is primary to the success of the program. The tenor of the evaluation becomes a function of supervisory-administrative behavior. The fundamental requisite for administrative behavior is consistency. Ambivalent behavior serves to cause a faculty to view the supervisor-administrator with suspicion. Effective teacher evaluation cannot become a reality in this setting. Thus, the supervisor is reminded that evaluation purpose should include:

1. Creating an environment for learning.
2. Providing assistance in selecting methods and materials to accomplish established behavioral objectives.
3. Initiating a quality supervisory program which supports self-improvement.
4. Behaving in such a manner that supervision is interpreted as being a cooperative function.
5. Developing a working environment whereby the faculty and auxiliary personnel work in professional security and confidence among and between faculty and supervisory personnel.

The supervisor-administrator must realize that by virtue of his position, the classroom teacher perceives him as

---

2. Ibid., pp. 314-316. Feyereisen et al. suggest that teacher preparation lacks required inclusion of measurement and evaluation. A program of in-service education might include: "preparation of tests and evaluation instruments; limitation of tests; interpreting test scores; diagnostic tests; basic statistical concepts and measurement; the purposes of the school system's evaluation program." (Reprinted by permission of Prentice-Hall, Inc., Englewood Cliffs, New Jersey.)

an authority figure. As an authority figure, his professional behavior should be above question and reflect judgment worthy of emulation. This aspect of the supervisory function is often overlooked. For the classroom teacher, self-concept and successful teaching experience are often a reflection of supervisory behavior. Thus, as the supervisor behaves, so does the faculty respond.

Basic to faculty response is supervisory attitude. Previously, flexible and rigid attitudes relative to problem-solving have been mentioned. In this case, the supervisory attitude interpreted by the faculty is what the supervisory attitude is regardless of what the supervisor's concept of this attitude may be. Supervisory-administrative behavior is as important to successful teacher evaluation as the making of correct judgments based upon documented evidence.

Summary

Teacher evaluation should be a systematic and continuous process with reference to the achievement of the objectives for a given school system. Even though a supervisor has been effective, there are dysfunctions within the work environment which serve to deter the quality of desired evaluative competence. Teacher evaluation is affected by the attitude of the supervisor and takes on special attributes of analysis with reference to his concept of measurement and evaluation. Cybernetic systems analysis, problem-solving, and feedback for self-improvement serve as fundamental means to bring about self-improvement. Teacher evaluation is as effective as the defined purpose for which evaluation is to serve. Thus, supervisory-administrative behavior emerges as a primary factor in successful teacher evaluation.

Major Themes

1. Supervision, measurement, and evaluation as defined by the supervisor-administrator are reflected in the act of teacher evaluation.
2. In spite of effective supervisory practice, dysfunctions are present which inhibit desired levels of supervisory competence.
3. Teacher evaluation is a continuous process.
4. Cybernetic systems analysis as a means of seeking solutions to identified problems in consonance with feedback is a viable means for self-improvement.
5. Teacher evaluation as a cooperative activity depends upon supervisory attitude.
6. Supervisory behavior is as important to successful teacher evaluation as the making of correct judgments based upon documented evidence.

Enrichment Readings

Lindemann, Bertram C., "Teacher Evaluation: Barrier to Communication?," Educational Leadership, Vol. 28 (November, 1970), pp. 207-208.

McNally, Harold J., "Teacher Evaluation That Makes a Difference," Educational Leadership, Vol. 29 (January, 1972), pp. 353-357.

Supplementary Readings

Arrigo, Frank, "How Was Your Write-UP?," High Points, Vol. 46 (October, 1964), pp. 65-66.

Campbell, David N., "A Report Card for Teachers," Pennsylvania School Journal, Vol. 120 (September, 1971), pp. 13-14.

Clement, Stanley L., "Why Is It? Teachers Shun Evaluation," Clearing House, Vol. 42 (April, 1968), pp. 465-467.

Delaney, Arthur A., "How to Kill a Good Teacher," Clearing House, Vol. 40 (April, 1966), pp. 504-506.

Flinker, Irving, "Reporting Teacher Observation," Clearing House, Vol. 41 (September, 1966), pp. 9-12.

Marshall, Max S., "Analyzing Evaluation," Educational Forum, Vol. 35 (May, 1971), pp. 487-490.

Musella, Donald, "Open-Closed-Mindedness as Related to the Rating of Teachers by Elementary School Principals," The Journal of Experimental Education, Vol. 35 (Spring, 1971), pp. 75-79.

Whippenpoof, Ezra B., "But Me No Buts," School and Community, Vol. 51 (May, 1965), pp. 42-43.

Chapter 8

EVALUATION OF INSTRUCTION

Formal Evaluation Procedure. Assuming that a school system has developed curriculum upon criterion performance objectives in consonance with a philosophy of education, the supervisor must be concerned with the evaluation of instruction. However, there is a need to describe the difference between the educator's concept of evaluation and the measurement specialist's concept of evaluation. One must also ascertain to what extent is ego satisfaction or protection of the offender found in dichotomizing the functional act of evaluation.

The concepts of the educator and the measurement specialist with reference to evaluation conceivably could be at variance. The gathered data per se is an expensive exercise and time consuming activity without the benefit of analysis for instructional modification. All too often, evaluation of instruction is based upon standardized tests and national norms.[1] Because these tests are based upon reading skills, the results may reflect reading facility rather than conceptual understanding and applied skills knowledge. These tests are administered to large groups of children which may be anxiety oriented. The question is one of such a test result being used in promotion, retention, and pupil grouping for instruction from remedial instruction to enrichment for the bright and gifted children. The supervisory-administrative personnel at the local school district

1. The authors are in no way discrediting standardized testing but the selection, purpose for administration, and use of data by local supervisory-administrative personnel is subject to serious question.

level have to resolve this basic issue before formal evaluation of instruction can begin.

A second aspect to be considered is the place of pupil achievement with reference to the evaluation of instruction. The wide range of uncontrollable variables[2] in any classroom environment serves to eliminate this statistical data for use in instructional evaluation. Thus, a program for instructional evaluation rests upon a resolution between the place of standardized statistical data and uncontrolled variables in the evaluation of instruction.

Using gathered data for analysis, identified instructional concern is quite different than labelling a level of instruction which may be a skewed mean or not applicable at the local attendance unit. This is dramatically seen where the attendance unit is predominantly bilingual. When recorded achievement is not what may be normally expected, the supervisor-administrator should answer the following questions:

1. Is the level of achievement realistic for this particular group of children?
2. Does the teacher have a variety of materials with which to provide personalized instruction?
3. Has the local classroom teacher been keeping evaluative data which could explain the reason for the less than anticipated achievement?
4. After checking previous supervisory reports could there be an instructional problem of which the teacher is not aware?
5. Is this group of children working with a pilot program?
6. Was the administered testing program appropriate for the intended results?

---

2. Uncontrollable instructional variables may include such items as: native ability, rate of learning assimilation, capacity to work with concrete and abstract information, and quality and amount of available instructional materials. This is not an exhaustive listing, only one that indicates factors at work in the instructional setting over which there is minimal or no control.

7. Has the computed data been checked for scoring, computation, and posting errors?

Once these questions have been answered it is time to develop a way to determine the problem focus and initiate means whereby instructional evaluation can be undertaken.

Teacher Observation--Fundamental to Evaluation. Fundamental to supervision is the observation of teachers in an instructional setting. Again, there is a basic position to be resolved because supervisor-administrators may be grouped into two behavioral patterns, the predictors and analysts. A predictor may be referred to as one who makes his judgments upon limited observational data, and the conclusions tend to be couched in suppositions. In contrast, an analyst perceives his decisions as being a result of systematic data gathering and continual review in terms of stated supervisory objectives.

Throughout all instructional evaluation activity, Lucio and McNeil state that the activity should concern itself with the extent to which specified predicted achievement was achieved, e.g., collect comprehensive evidence or sample pupil behavior required by the stated instructional objectives in all situations in which the behavior is expected to apply. Attention should be given to both expected and unexpected behavior.[3] Also, the evaluator should be able to record data with a variety of measures which accurately describe the learning that was intended--did it occur and if not why not--and determine what steps toward refinement are required.[4]

Mid Course Corredia

The actual supervisory observation, like the supervisory conference, should be mutually planned by teacher and supervisor. How the observation will be conducted and what will be included in the time to be observed becomes the focus of planning. In the planning session, the teacher and the super-

---

3. William H. Lucio and John D. McNeil. Supervision: A Synthesis of Thought and Action. New York: McGraw-Hill Book Company, 1962, p. 248.

4. Ibid.

visor-administrator can gain insight into the problem focus if answers to the following questions can be determined:

1. Would greater opportunity to respond actively in the learning situations have improved results?

2. Would more opportunity for the pupils to practice both prerequisite and final behavior have changed the outcome of instruction.

3. Would greater provision for individual differences in interest, ability, or prior achievement have had an effect on the learner's behavior?

4. Would more emphasis on the purpose of the instructional unit have changed the learner's behavior?

5. Would modification of the rate of presentation and time allowed for response of the learner have influenced his performance?[5]

The emphasis is placed upon teacher behavior in terms of pupil learning and the pupil's response to that behavior in the instructional setting. In the past, the lack of pupil success, or limited success, has been described as something wrong with the learner. Then as now, this is an indefensible position for any teacher to take because his responsibility is to instruct regardless of the students assigned to him. When a pupil is blamed for his lack of success it indicates that the teacher and possibly the supervisor-administrator have not gotten to the basis of the problem or they have relied totally on statistical information. An area often overlooked as a deterrent to learning is the child's world outside of the school and its effect upon learning. Within this framework, attitudes which the child brings to school are very difficult to ascertain, and their effect on pupil performance is next to impossible to evaluate. However, the

---

5. Ibid., p. 249.

outside world of the learner is a factor that cannot be dismissed lightly.

Assuming that the learner will not be blamed for his level of success and responsibility for that performance is accepted by both the instructional and supervisory personnel, the teacher and supervisor-administrator should attempt to find answers to the following questions in preparation for the observation session:

1. Do I know what is to be taught? Have I selected valid instructional objectives?
2. How can I best teach to achieve the instructional objectives?
3. Have I planned for ordering the presentation of contents?
4. Have I established criterion measures which will indicate successful attainment of the objectives?[6]

These questions get to the central issue of instruction. When teachers can provide acceptable answers to these questions, then pupil behavior can be more accurately appraised for modification and personalization of instruction. (Appendix H.) To bring this full cycle, the supervisor-administrator has a set of questions which he must answer so that he can more accurately evaluate teacher instruction. These questions are:

1. Have I helped the teacher to view supervision as a technical resource designed to help him achieve the objectives of the school?
2. Is there conscientious attention on the part of the teacher to support the objectives of the school?
3. Have the motives which caused the teacher to enter teaching and the motives which currently sustain him emerged in our person-to-person relations? If these motives were

6. *Ibid.*, pp. 254-255.

assessed negatively, e.g., a temporary career interest, has the teaching experience developed an awareness of professional responsibility on the part of the teacher?

4. Have I controlled my bias against those aspects of the teacher's personality which were at variance with my expectations but which do not relate to, or stand in the way of, competent teaching performance?

5. Has the teacher met the agreed-upon criterion for achievement in spite of what might seem to others undesirable personality traits or the application of unique or "different" classroom teaching procedures? In other words, do criterion measures show that the teacher's methods of instruction have resulted in positive educative experiences for pupils?[7]

Evaluation of instruction should be a continuous cooperative effort between the classroom teacher and the supervisor-administrator. This evaluation should be an on-going activity in terms of the educational objectives set forth for the course of study being instructed. Final analysis must be in terms of whether or not the instructional objectives were accomplished. Attitudes toward teacher style and supervisory and teacher bias must be relegated to their proper perspectives when instruction is being evaluated. Although instructional evaluation is primarily a function of teacher-supervisory planning, the learner should have an opportunity to evaluate his own performance. In so doing, the professional staff should make every effort to have the learner's responses concern themselves with acquired learning versus commentary on teacher style and personality. Granted, teacher style and personality are factors of successful instruction, but the learners should confine their responses to the acquisition of knowledge. Input from each of these three sources should provide valuable insight into the level of effective instruction in any public or private school system.

---

7. *Ibid*.

Summary

Evaluation of instruction becomes a planned activity between the supervisor-administrator and the classroom teacher. Character of the evaluation takes on the philosophy and values of the supervisor-administrator who may be evaluation or measurement oriented. Within this framework, the supervisory-administrative behavior dictates the quality of observation and overgeneralizes, whereas the analyst gathers data and more objectively arrives at his professional conclusions. The supervisory observation, like the supervisory conferences, must focus upon planning and follow-up activity which is acceptable to both the teacher being observed and the supervisor in consonance with the educational objectives of the school system. Evaluation of instruction must be made in terms of whether or not the objectives of the observed instruction were accomplished.

Major Themes

1. Instructional evaluation quality is reflected by the educator's and measurement specialist's concepts of evaluation.
2. A program of instructional evaluation rests upon a resolution between the place of standardized statistical data and uncontrolled variables in the evaluation of instruction.
3. Standardized tests may not provide an accurate measurement in atypical attendance units, e.g., bilingual concentration.
4. Instructional evaluation and teacher observation are fundamental to the supervisory function.
5. The quality of instructional evaluation will vary in terms of whether the evaluator's behavior is one of a predictor or an analyst.

6. The observation session, like the supervisory conference, should be mutually planned with both the classroom teacher and the supervisor.
7. Final analysis must be in terms of whether or not the instructional objectives were accomplished.
8. The learner should be provided with an opportunity to participate in instructional evaluation.

Enrichment Readings

Curtin, James, and Stanley Gilbertson, "The Principal and the Instructional Program," National Elementary Principal," Vol. 45 (September, 1965), pp. 53-55.

Supplementary Readings

Gerber, Murray B., and John Henry Martin, "How to Keep Teachers on the Ball," School Management, Vol. 10 (March, 1966), pp. 94-98, 180-183.

Giles, Douglas E., "Catalyst or Supressant to Dynamic Teaching?" Childhood Education, Vol. 43 (January, 1967), pp. 289-291.

Huenecke, Dorothy, "Knowledge of Curriculum Works: Its Relation to Teaching Practice," Journal of Teacher Education, Vol. 21 (Winter, 1970), pp. 478-483.

Peterson, Janet A., "The Principal Influences Learning," Educational Leadership, Vol. 23 (February, 1966), pp. 409-415.

Stufflebeam, Daniel L., "The Use of Experimental Design in Educational Evaluation," Journal of Educational Measurement, Vol. 8 (Winter, 1971), pp. 267-274.

Wey, Herbert W., "The Principal and Quality Education," Phi Delta Kappan, Vol. 46 (December, 1964), pp. 178-180.

Chapter 9

EVALUATION OF EDUCATIONAL CHANGE PROCESS

Elements Necessary for Evaluation. Now that curriculum and teacher competence have been the focal point, supervision must be subject to evaluation. Reflecting upon the focus of supervisory intent, Curtin suggests that three emphases should be considered when evaluating supervision: (1) procedures as well as outcomes, (2) supervision as a part of a total process concerned with the improvement of instruction, and (3) supervision with reference to its intended purposes.[1] Within this framework, he suggests that five conditions must exist before effective evaluation of supervision can take place. These include: (1) accessibility to data, (2) an attitude which is evaluation oriented, (3) continuous communication between supervisors and teachers, (4) teachers free from administrative threat and/or intimidation, and (5) enough time to perform the evaluation task.[2] Upon reviewing these components necessary for evaluation, those concerned with evaluation must be cognizant of the interdependence of each component. At the same time, two factors overlooked are: (1) freedom from threat and/or intimidation and (2) enough time to perform the evaluation task.

Many an administrator-supervisor will state that his faculty are free to express their professional judgments; however, when this is taken literally by a faculty member, there is a tendency for the supervisor to find himself labelled a "trouble maker," and "upstart," "presumptuous," and

---

1. James Curtin. Supervision in Today's Elementary School. New York: The Macmillan Company, 1964, p. 278.

2. Ibid., pp. 278-279.

a myriad of other descriptive adjectives. Some might think such faculty behavior is naive, especially for the beginning classroom teacher. Yet, it is the beginning, non-tenured faculty member who may be anxious to work and try new methods and techniques of instruction. He is eager to implement that which he has acquired as a part of his professional preparation. The probationary classroom teacher sincerely tries to assist and work for the improvement of curriculum and often meets cynical attitudes from more experienced teachers. This type of response tends to undermine the insecure, discourage the able, and cause others to leave the profession. Also, a great many others, who work diligently to "keep school," knuckle under and fall victim to the administrator-supervisor. Within this context, evaluation of supervision is most difficult, because in this setting supervision ceases to exist and dictatorial measures reign.

On the other hand, a few administrators who supervise do exercise educational statesmanship and do create an atmosphere supported by their own behavior whereby an individual faculty member will freely make adjustments, disagree, and become involved in a discussion which leads to the resolution of professional differences. Those who have the ability to develop and sustain effective leadership qualities should be successful in the supervisory role.

Evaluation of supervision takes time. If evaluation is accepted as a continuous process, then adequate time for evaluation must be provided within the school calendar. Data gathering is a basic activity; however, the analysis of collected data is a time-consuming activity. This is the challenge which confronts the evaluation of supervision. Analysis of the data must be in terms of the designated purposes of the supervisory program.

Evaluation Made in Context of Purpose. Not unlike the evaluation of curriculum and teacher competence to instruct effectively, evaluation must be undertaken in terms of purpose. Examination of the supervisory function gives the parameters of purpose to be evaluated. In effect, the question revolves about the degree to which supervisory personnel are involved in administrative decision-making including: (1) providing a proper classroom environment, (2) supplying methods and materials to insure a personalized orientation to curriculum, (3) providing a supervisory program to attain instructional goals, (4) developing an attitude among the staff that supervision must be a cooperative participation between the classroom teacher and supervisor-administrator, (5) developing an attitude that perceives instructional improvement as being directly related to self-improvement, (6) providing specific help to teachers with day-to-day problems, and (7) providing a professional climate which promotes security and confidence among faculty members.

Self-evaluation of the Supervisor-Administrator. Regardless of the means by which supervision is evaluated, the primary evaluation rests in the integrity of an intelligent supervisor-administrator by his evaluation of his own work. In retrospect, the authors stated that the supervisory personality was a primary factor in effective supervision programming. Likewise, supervisory personality becomes a significant factor in self-evaluation. For the overall good of the school district, self-evaluation must be truthfully objective and above trivia which tends to be centered upon the petty and mundane. Yet, evaluation must be undertaken by "outsiders," i.e., those who are affected by the supervisory process. In reality, an evaluation by others tends to effect change whereas self-analysis that is not honest makes all other attempts at evaluation meaningless.

One means of self-evaluation is to ask others. Teachers observe supervisors every day and have frequent contact with them. Thus, this large source of information often provides invaluable insight relative to the supervisor's professional behavior which he can use to interpret his strengths and weaknesses. When requesting information from the instructional faculty, it is important that the questions are phrased in such a manner that the response will be directly to the point of the information sought. Teachers might respond to questions which concern themselves with: (1) supervisory strengths, (2) supervisory limitations, (3) suggestions for improvement, and (4) suggestions for additional types of help not currently incorporated in the program of supervision at the local level.

Another source of information is the parents of the pupils of the local attendance unit. Although parents may not be curriculum specialists nor established scholars, they do have attitudes about the curriculum presented at the local school level where their children are educated. When evaluating parental response, it should be as a subtle response to their likes and dislikes. Most important in this type of response are the areas of complaint and the incidence of the complaint registered. This type of response provides an indirect means for evaluating the ongoing program.

In self-evaluation, there may be a tendency to use the pragmatic "soul searching" approach; however, self-evaluation must be based upon solid evidence. Finally, it must be noted that supervision in practice is not amenable to elementary analysis. Therefore, when evaluating supervision, primary attention should be given to the collection of evidence. One factor which must be kept in mind is that evaluative instruments should not be allowed to obscure the complexity of the evaluation process. This is particularly true of supervisory attempts with self-evaluation. (Appendix I.)

Fundamental to self-evaluation is the interpersonal relationships of the professional staff which serve to effect the evaluation process. Berlin and Wyckoff[3] suggest aims which assist in helping two persons do better work in a cooperative professional manner.

> Two individuals working together with the material must confront it together. Four general aims underlie the approach:
>
> 1. To deepen one's ability to be more aware of his own feelings and the feelings of others;

---

3. Role of Supervisor and Curriculum Director in a Climate of Change, ASCD Yearbook. Washington, D.C.: Association for Supervision and Curriculum Development, 1965, p. 162.

2. To enhance one's appreciation of his own potential;

3. To increase flexibility in both the emotional and cognitive aspects of behavior;

4. To develop the ability to apply these new behavior patterns to the life situation.[4]

In the final analysis, in order to effectuate continual leadership in a time of change and uncertainty, the supervisor-administrator must be cognizant of three basic needs: (1) the need to project a clear picture of specialized professional functions, (2) the need to develop more adequate conceptual tools to carry out unique professional functions, and (3) the need to cultivate openness to new experiences.[5]

Summary

Evaluation of educational change process--supervision--should be a continuous activity where the faculty have an opportunity to make a contribution free from professional reprisal. Two factors often neglected when evaluating supervision are the acquisition of accurate data and its analysis in terms of designated purposes. Without purpose, evaluation cannot be undertaken. The areas which must be considered when evaluating the supervisor-administrator on his ability to accurately assess need and make a significant contribution in those administrative decisions which affect curriculum development and teacher instructional competence.

Self-evaluation of the supervisor-administrator is desirable; however, "soul searching" must be substituted with evidence. The instructional faculty remains the best source of information whereby the supervisor-administrator can interpret the success of his supervisory program. In-

---

4. Ibid.

5. Ibid., p. 163

creased interpersonal relationships which emphasize positive leadership--a leadership which clearly explains the specialized openness--combine to create a cooperative relationship whereby the supervisor-administrator can effectively carry out his program and have it accepted by the instructional faculty at the local level of both public and private educational systems.

Major Themes

1. Elements necessary for evaluation should be centered around procedures and outcomes, a part of instructional improvement, and evaluation in terms of purpose.
2. Evaluation which is meaningful depends upon criteria which must be held inviolate: (1) accessibility to data, (2) continuous communication between supervisor and teacher, (3) an attitude which is evaluation oriented, (4) teachers free from administrative threat and/or intimidation, and (5) enough time to perform the evaluation task.
3. Evaluation of supervision must be made in the context of purpose.
4. Self-evaluation of the supervisor-administrator is desirable and encouraged.
5. Self-evaluation must be based upon evidence.
6. The instructional faculty are the largest and best informed source to evaluate the supervisor-administrator's work.
7. Parents have specific attitudes about their children's education, and they should be allowed to register their concerns.
8. Increased interpersonal relationship insures a greater degree of supervisory-administrative acceptance by the faculty and associated personnel.
9. Successful supervisory leadership must function in a time of continual change and uncertainty.

Enrichment Readings

Mosher, Lillian I., "The Supervisor Looks at the Principal," Educational Leadership, Vol. 23 (May, 1966), pp. 648-651.

Supplementary Readings

Chesler, M., and Robert Fox, "Teacher Peer Relations and Educational Change," NEA Journal, Vol. 56 (May, 1967), pp. 25-26.

Denny, Robert, "A Rating Scale for Elementary Principals," American School Board Journal, Vol. 149 (December, 1964), pp. 11-12.

Howsam, Robert B., and John M. Franco, "New Emphases in Evaluation of Administrators," National Elementary Principal, Vol. 44 (April, 1965), pp. 36-40.

Hughes, L. W., and C. M. Achilles, "The Supervisor as a Change Agent," Educational Leadership, Vol. 28 (May, 1971), pp. 840-843.

Michaud, Arnaud, E., "How to Evaluate Your Nonteaching Staff Members--and Make Them Like It," School Management, Vol. 10 (November, 1966), pp. 86-92.

Osborne, Grace S., and Allan S. Hurlburt, "Credibility Gap in Supervision," School and Society, Vol. 99 (November, 1971), pp. 415-417.

Appendixes

Appendix A

SPECIFIC ACTIVITIES FOR PURPOSEFUL INVOLVEMENT

A Preferred Situation--Professional Assignment. To begin with, a supervisor without a job description is working with a handicap. An added problem exists when a building principal assumes supervisory duties. The recommended relationship might more appropriately be that the principal remain on the line staff, but that the supervisor be taken off the line staff organization in the administration of a school district. In fact, curriculum development and in-service programs have suffered immeasurable damage when a building principal and supervisor have been in professional conflict. This conflict usually takes the form of: (1) a principal's feeling threatened that his professional leadership is being challenged, (2) supervisory anxiety which continually escalates because of his not being able to carry out planned programs, and (3) supervisor-teacher interpersonal relationships where a hypercritical supervisor indiscriminately criticizes classroom teachers at work.

Ideally, the building principal should concern himself with the management of the school building, and the supervisor should be responsible for curriculum development and its implementation. The supervisor's recommendations should be reported directly to the Assistant Superintendent for Curriculum who is responsible for the professional behavior of the principal at the local attendance unit. Accountability then is to the assistant superintendent for both the principal and supervisor. He can act as an arbitrator should differences in analysis and recommended programming develop. (See Figure A-1.)

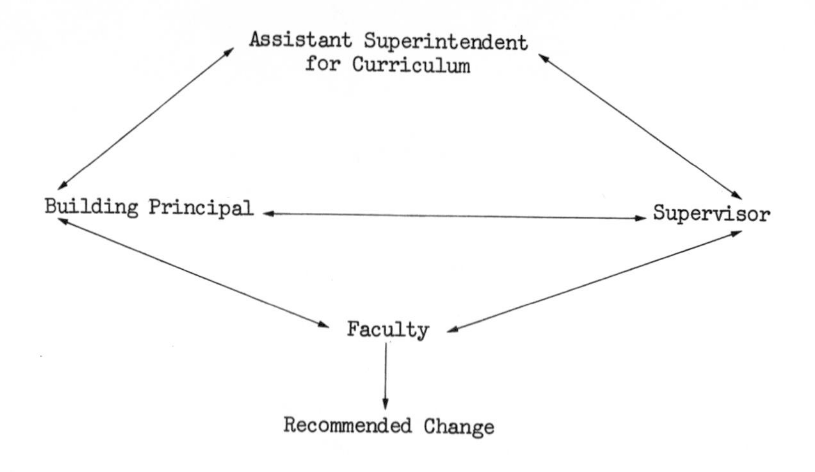

Fig. A-1

RECOMMENDED AUTHORITY LINE

Activities for Purposeful Involvement--Survey. At the pre-school workshop or at the close of the school year in May or June, a questionnaire should be administered which requests information concerning suggested activity and willingness to participate in differentiated work assignments. Upon completion of the questionnaire analysis, a supervisor has immediate access to workshop leadership potential at the local level. (See Figure A-2.)

Supervisory-Faculty Relationship. By scheduled appointment, the supervisor should take time to counsel with the faculty and staff and genuinely take them into his confidence. All too often the supervisor "talks" and the faculty acquiesces to the dictates of a supervisor versus a program resulting from a combined professional effort. The faculty and staff should be guided, assisted, and encouraged as well as systematically evaluated throughout curriculum development and in-service participation. When evaluated work is not acceptable, the question technique allows a faculty member to explain his behavior. This approach to problem-solving provides the faculty member an opportunity to "save face."

Counsel can be undertaken tactfully, without embarassment, in a closed conference session. (See Figure A-3.)

SURVEY QUESTIONNAIRE

Name ____
(Last) (First)

Address ____
(Street) (City-Village) (State-Zip)

Telephone ______________________ Instructional area _____
(Area Code) (Number)

Academic Preparation

College-University	Degree/Certification	Date
______________	______________	____
______________	______________	____
______________	______________	____

Workshop Attendance (Last three years)

Place attended	Topic	Date
____________	__________________________	____
____________	__________________________	____
____________	__________________________	____
____________	__________________________	____
____________	__________________________	____
____________	__________________________	____

Curriculum Development
In-service

Check the appropriate response with an (X).

1. Would you be willing to participate in an in-service program? Yes ___ No ___
2. Would you consent to work on a curriculum task force in an instructional area? Yes ___ No ___

3. Would you participate in a pilot project?
   Yes ___ No ___
4. Would you be willing to participate in a research project? Yes ___ No ___
5. Would you be willing to participate in the development of evaluation instruments for both students and faculty? Yes ___ No ___

Fig. A-2

SAMPLE EVALUATIVE STATEMENTS AND QUESTIONS

Statements--Positive in Orientation

1. These objectives clearly follow the school's philosophy of education.
2. The classroom management was accurately designed for the intended instruction (small group).
3. The increased use of hardware (be specific) has allowed for more opportunity to personalize curriculum.

Questions of Negative Orientation

1. How were these objectives developed?
2. Do these evaluation instruments really test the objectives?
3. Does this activity really provide enrichment or more of the same?

Fig. A-3

Purposeful Delegation of Authority. Analysis of the questionnaire data provides information for purposeful delegation of authority within the ongoing program of supervision. First, those persons who are willing to participate in the in-service assignments are identified. Second, those persons who exhibit a willingness to accept leadership assignments are identified. Unless the supervisor utilizes the data, he will be accused of involving the faculty without purpose.

Selection of Consultants. During the past two decades there has been a tendency to overuse consultants in a program of in-service education at the local school level. Often these consultants do not have effective briefing prior to their visits, and as a result, their contributions sometimes cause more trouble than they are worth. Also, there is a tendency for consultants to be initiators, exploding with ideas; however, once they have left the local scene, their proposals and initiated action have limited carry-over and follow-through activity. Consultants should be employed to undertake specific activities which are known to the faculty in advance. Assuming consultants have desired expertise, their ability to relate effectively to and with a faculty is essential. An antagonistic consultant should be avoided.

Many school faculties have qualified faculty who can function in the consultant role. Much energy and talent await encouragement and development at the local school district level. One important function of supervision is the development of leadership within the local school system.

Credibility in Jeopardy. Regretfully, man as supervisor-administrator realizes too late that his credibility is in question, literally, and his basic professional behavior is suspect. This situation comes into being when the supervisor-administrator (1) plays "games," (2) shows overt favoritism, (3) relies on the faculty to supply opinionated data relative to faculty and staff rather than keeping his associations and questions in the academic sector, (4) exhibits a dichotomy between word and deed, (5) deliberately manipulates the faculty to superimpose curriculum development and in-service activity upon the faculty, and (6) is continually at variance with administration. The effective supervisor-administrator must be above suspicion and have a reputation for unquestioned integrity. He must be able to work with the total faculty as well as create and sustain instructional leadership. At the same time, the supervisor-administrator has to keep each component functioning with the philosophy of the school district coupled with priority designation perspective. In the final analysis, a supervisor-administrator must be a disciplined educational statesman.

Appendix B

EVALUATION IN SUPERVISION

Accountability. Supervision no longer is immune from evaluation. Within this program, a professional educator must be able to demonstrate his competence in instructional method and technique which is reflected in pupil behavior. In order to achieve this objective, a supervisor-administrator must have the authority to develop, select, and administer both formal and informal instruments designed to evaluate instructional effectiveness.

Although emphasis is often placed upon the evaluation of instructional competence among the faculty, it is equally important that the supervisory personnel (supervisors and principals who perform supervisory duties) be able to accurately observe and interpret what they observe. All too often, the building principal who is assigned to evaluate teacher instructional competence may have no professional expertise in the using of evaluation instruments. Therefore, the procedure and technique of evaluation to be utilized by the supervisory personnel should be included in the in-service program at the beginning of the school year. At that time, sessions for administrators and faculty should be held both separately and jointly in order that the faculty and administrators as a whole can be specifically informed about: (1) instruments to be used, (2) format in which each will be utilized, (3) who will administer, review, and interpret results, (4) how the results will be recorded, (5) purpose of the pre- and post-conferences, and (6) the twofold purpose of the evaluation process--to improve instruction for the pupils and to insure continuity of curriculum within the educational objectives and philosophy of a local school system.

Informal Instruments. Many public and private school faculties are committed now to personalizing their curriculum. There is an attempt to provide for individual differences by prescriptive design. In order to achieve this goal, a team of faculty members could develop a check list of behavioral outcomes with an assigned rating scale for the purpose of informal evaluation. Such a listing can be one of self-analysis or one administered by an observer.

Another rating scale which can be helpful, administered informally, or in a formal procedure, is Coody and Harris' inventory entitled How Well Is Instruction Being Individualized?[1] Twenty items relative to instruction, technique, classroom management, and materials utilization are rated from a maximum of 5 to a low of 1. An analysis of this inventory data provides an individual classroom teacher as well as the supervisor with an index insight into a teacher's attitude toward instruction of an individual, regardless of the subject matter or grade-level placement.

For ready reference, a sample from the Coody-Harris inventory has been included for examination.[2]

		5	4	3	2	1
a.	Pupils do advanced level of enrichment.	Nearly half of the pupils do obviously advanced level or enrichment work.		Several pupils do advanced level or enrichment work.		No pupil does advanced or enrichment work.
f.	Pupils work independently in intraclass groups.	Pupils work in small groups with little direction for prolonged periods of time.		Most pupils work independently in small groups for short periods of time.		Pupils work in small or large groups under the direction of the teacher at all times.
t.	Pupils are held responsible for their actions.	The teacher leaves the pupils free to carry out assignments independently.		The teacher gives advice to pupils while assignments are being carried out.		The teacher closely directs, checks, and advises pupils while assignments are being carried out.

1. Betty Coody and Ben M. Harris. How Well Is Instruction Being Individualized?, ICIM Service Bureau, University of Texas, Austin, 1965.

2. Ibid.

Formal Evaluation Instruments. The VTR (Video Tape Recorder) has become an evaluative device which brings documented proof to the act of evaluation. This device has yet to be utilized with systematic planning on a mass scale. Like the planning for a supervisory conference and teacher-observation conference, planning for a taping session should focus upon one aspect of instructional competency and/or associated skills. The video-taped sessions provide visual documentation for analysis and counsel, in contrast to a myriad of general and often meaningless comments. Because building principals are still delegated supervisory duties, their orientation to video taping and follow-up coding and interpretation should be a primary emphasis in all supervisory programs regardless of the district size.[3]

Many supervisory personnel use a check list as a means for evaluation during the observation sessions. These sessions tend to be infrequent and not always "scheduled" during the three- to five-year probationary period. The conference accompanying these observation sessions may or may not have been held. Thus, there seems to be no consistent follow through on the part of those undertaking supervision duties. Of specific importance is that the reports filed by the supervisor often have a direct effect upon whether or not a teacher receives reappointment, or a continuing contract.

Unfortunately, the format of many evaluation check lists still contains terminology or their semantic equivalents such as: "poor, average, good, very good, and excellent." As a result, the statements become general to the point that the evaluated teacher leaves a follow-up conference or reacts to a letter with disdain because there is little or no specific

---

3. A successful in-service program focusing on the use of the VTR as an evaluation tool in supervision involving administrators was designed by Mr. Noel Jackson, Assistant Superintendent for Curriculum, Harlingen ISD, Harlingen, Texas, and Dr. David L. Zufelt, Associate Professor of Education, Texas A and I University at Kingsville. The program features a five-module sequence with workshop and associated follow-up activity. Additional information can be obtained by writing to Mr. Jackson.

information which evaluates his instructional competence let alone providing suggestions for improvement where appropriate.

In contrast, the VTR, coupled with interaction-analysis coding, provides for a systematic and organized interpretation based upon stated criteria. Once again, the faculty must be made aware of the specific outcomes desired by the supervisory personnel and for what purpose the tapes will be utilized if kept on file for comparative analysis. When programmed VTR and appropriate conferencing become scheduled by design, the tapes and written analyses provide for a continuum of performance accountability which heretofore has not been characteristic of supervisory evaluation.[4]

---

4. The authors have emphasized the use of the inventory analysis and VTR competency evaluation because, with a minimum of in-service instruction, personnel can learn to apply coding techniques and interpret with accuracy. Thus, the subjectivity which characterized supervision of the past can be diminished if not eliminated.

Appendix C

ORIENTATION REFLECTS FACULTY-STAFF PARTICIPATION

Preplanning Not Enough. Presupposing that professional planning has taken place, this mechanical scheduling of people, places, and things is not enough to insure continual success for in-service faculty-staff programs. Like a catalytic agent, pre-in-service orientation is essential. Identification of terminal objectives as it relates to participant behavior is vital to the success of the program.

A fundamental miscalculation of supervisor-administrators is that they assume that the faculty and staff know what will be expected of them. Supervisory personnel seem to assume that the in-service programs, of both short- and long-range duration, are self-explanatory. On the contrary, the authors have observed many in-service programs which are less than goal oriented, let alone having relevance to a planned program of supervision. Likewise, few in-service programs seem to be planned in consonance with a philosophy of education associated with skill competencies. In effect, many in-service programs are aimless gatherings of circular verbal motion ending with unresolved issues. Many a curriculum guide was written for accreditation, never to be implemented in the instructional setting. It is no wonder that in-service education programs have been and continue to be evaluated by many as a "waste of time." In-service education in many school systems has succumbed to the committee syndrome.

Faculty-Staff Participation. Faculty-staff participation in an in-service program is basically one of forced duty as opposed to participation with an attitude of being assisted in performing professional work at an increased level of competence. Fundamental to basic administration is the clarification of objectives which are explained in advance to the participants. These objectives should be in two different forms of orientation: (1) supervisory-administrative which reflects public and private school philosophy and management policy and (2) specific behavioral outcomes for the faculty and staff. Knowing what can be expected allows the participants an opportunity to be intelligent participants rather than disinterested, passive participants.

Total Faculty-Staff Sessions Overdone. Basic to in-service programming is the organizational format. Observation by the authors shows a trend for large group sessions dominated by guest speakers who comment on lofty topics which have little or no relevance to local concerns. Little is accomplished in assisting those in attendance with solving problems. It is suggested that more vigorous participation would be forthcoming from faculty and staff if emphasis were placed on small-group work sessions. In this setting, local problems can be solved. The participants identify with specific problems, but have difficulty relating to issues outside of their professional assignment. Thus, small-group sessions with specific subject orientation hold promise for meaningful resolution as opposed to the continuum of all faculty-staff sessions.

Follow-up Essential for Sustained Quality Participation. Conversation with numerous faculty and staff members reveals a silent pessimism to the point of indifference toward follow-up and eventual implementation of programs related to supervision. For many, a progress report would have been appreciated which told the status of programs. For others, indifference was the result of decisions being overruled by the central office administration. When this arbitrary action is perpetrated by the supervisory personnel, soon a "no confidence" attitude prevails. Once this has happened, the supervisory personnel should consider seeking other employment because effectiveness as instructional leaders has terminated at a given school district.

A supervisor-administrator who wishes to insure sustained quality participation by faculty and staff will consistently:

(1) notify in-service participants in advance of the objectives to be obtained during the sessions, (2) specifically state what the participants can expect to receive from their input, and (3) notify faculty and staff periodically about the status of programs and their implementation as it reflects participant recommendation and/or decisions. The supervisory personnel have the obligation to inform the faculty and staff as to why recommendations and decisions have not been made operative. The quality of faculty-staff participation in in-service programs hinges upon a continuous orientation to the purpose and anticipated outcomes with reference to instructional improvement.

Appendix D

SUPERIMPOSITION WITHOUT MODIFICATION

Money and More Money. The "golden age" of the past decade provided an almost unlimited amount of federal support whereby school district personnel could purchase the services of professional faculty, supportive staffing, as well as software and hardware for the purpose of instructional improvement. Money was used to shore up old programs with new technology. Old programs and new technology, coupled with the same supervisory personnel and instructional faculty, do not necessarily produce effective educational experiences. Availability of additional financial aid through federal support has not changed the quality of education for numerous children throughout the nation.

Industry Can Only Assist. Research undertaken by educators at the university level has found its way into programs and instructional materials. The market has been flooded with both hardware and software, so much so that the classroom teacher and supervisor have difficulty keeping account of what is available. With all of this assistance to aid in personalizing curriculum, many a classroom teacher resists the utilization of such common instructional assists as the overhead projector, movies, filmstrips, and programmed instruction. Worse yet, many of these same teachers show no inclination to learn how to use these materials for instructional improvement, but claim to be concerned about teaching the individual child. As a result, supervisory-administrative personnel have made arbitrary decisions to implement such programs as modern mathematics, linguistics, process approach in science, and a course of study in social studies. Often, success is minimal because these programs are being implemented in a haphazard fashion by faculty and aides who do not comprehend the mechanics of instructional management and/or its content. Thus, teachers' manuals and workbooks continue to reign in many classrooms throughout the nation where teachers remain the central focus and children continue to be passive learners.

A Need to Reeducate or Replace. Teachers with a span of four decades of teacher education are practicing the art of instruction in the nation's schools. The educator, regardless of his age or preparation, has continued to prepare himself to meet new instructional challenges. Concern is expressed for those who view their work as a second income, or those who feel that the "status quo" is good enough. The teachers who feel no responsibility to keep acquiring new methods and techniques to improve their instructional competence must now come to grips with accountability. With a surplus of teachers throughout the nation, how long will local school district administrators allow a teacher to remain who exhibits this attitude toward instruction? Accountability requirements may force both administrators and teachers to retire early. In addition, revision in school policy concerning issuance of continuing appointments may serve to cause a large annual turnover in personnel. Accountability requirements may also be reflected in a reexamination of tenure. Thus, the classroom teachers and administrators who do not professionally continue to improve their instructional competence may be eliminated from the rank and file of professional educators.

Appendix E

FOLLOW-UP

Positive Statement. When beginning the follow-up, the supervisor should be tactful and begin with a positive statement. The initial statement is crucial to the teacher who has been observed because he will interpret the statement as a reflection of supervisory attitude. For example:

1. "Your purpose was clearly expressed and emphasized when you utilized the bulletin board as an applied visual aid."
2. "One of the strengths of your lesson was the tactfulness which you demonstrated in handling Ken's incorrect response without making him appear unworthy in front of his peers."
3. "Your preparation with documented data, cumulative file, and anecdotal records clearly illustrated Jean's inability to get along with her classmates. Your suggestion and request for parents' assistance showed genuine concern for this child."

Supervisory attitude that is sharply critical can quickly undermine the observed teacher. When a teacher interprets supervisory commentary as consistently being helpful, receptiveness for meaningful change has been enhanced.

Comment Only on Known Data. When conducting a follow-up conference, a supervisor should avoid mentioning information that cannot be substantiated by recorded data. Comments beginning with the following introductory phrases should be avoided:

1. "I think . . ."
2. "It would appear . . ."
3. "In my opinion . . ."
4. "Miss X thinks . . ."

5. "There ought to have been . . ."

These introductory phrases suggest opinion, subjective judgment, and hearsay and in general allude to generalizations which do not give the observed teacher specific information. On the other hand, it suggests that the supervisor is unwilling to be specific. This in turn has a tendency to be a factor in which the supervisor loses the respect of the faculty and associated personnel.

Criticism Should Be Tentative. There is a tendency to couch supervisory commentary in such language that it could be interpreted that the condition and/or situation could not be improved or modified. All evaluative statements might well begin with such phrases as:

1. "At this time . . ."
2. "With practice . . ."
3. "A change in classroom management will . . ."

As a result, the listener realizes that supervisory statements are focused upon the time of the observation and must be kept in that context. Suggested means for change in effect illustrate the tentativeness of the supervisor's commentary. The comments stated in a follow-up conference should not be interpreted as an indictent. When this happens, the supervisor will have a next to impossible task regaining confidence in perceiving him in the role of a sincere helper.

Be Aware of Communication Tone. Whether in written form or in conversation, the choice of vocabulary and delivery is very important. How information is presented may be more important than what is said. The supervisory-personality is determined by the tone of word choice. Written communication is difficult for most supervisors, and the following guidelines are provided as a suggested format:

1. To make a statement of positive commentary.
2. To isolate a specific problem within the context of agreed-upon content of the observation.
3. To recall specific suggestions.
4. To close with a statement of encouragement.

5. To make a statement requesting alternative times when the supervisor would be able to come for professional assistance again.

Appendix F

SOLUTION TO IDENTIFIED PROBLEMS

Identified Problems Must Be Realistic. Identification of serious problems is essential if solution serves to affect the total improvement of the education system at the local level. From a questionnaire, areas of concern are identified. Within this framework, the supervisor can be an agent who can guide the faculty in the establishment of a priority which is realistic for the district. Realistic problem consideration must concern itself with such factors as:

1. Elements of fad or fashion.
2. How many children and/or young adults are affected.
3. The available sources on site.
4. The amount needed--hardware and software--with appropriate costs.
5. The amount and kind of in-service education for faculty, aides, and staff.
6. Community attitude and willingness to support.
7. Immediateness of the problem.

Of these factors, community attitude and its willingness to provide support for projects and new or modified programs is often underestimated. Herein lies the fundamental element of public relations which is often neglected prior to initiating any selected program.

Flexible Alternatives. When a problem has been identified, there is a tendency for a committee to decide which procedure and materials will be used. The committee's decision is not the point in question, but the additional aspects of problem-solving which many supervisors overlook when they do not involve members of the faculty. Even though a plan of action has been agreed upon, alternatives should also be planned. Alternative planning before the initiation of a project is the key to flexibility. Alternative planning also implies that continuous evaluation is taking place.

Continuous Evaluation. The supervisor has the responsibility for continuous evaluation. One aspect of this evaluation often overlooked is the judgment of the involved faculty. All too often, the evaluation of progress is observed and described from the central-office point of view. Valuable insight is lost when the classroom teacher who deals with the instructional problems everyday is not allowed to participate in the drafting of the final evaluation statement so that it represents both supervisory and instructional input.

In the Final Analysis. Solving an identified problem is not so much an academic process as it is one of selecting means by which to solve the problem. Once the problem has been identified, the challenge is one of coordinating diverse personality and hidden agendas which require the continued best of supervisory statesmanship.

Appendix G

EFFECTIVE TEACHER EVALUATION

Limit Scope of Involvement. A supervisor can best serve his professional work if he will take the time to clarify the parameters of his position. The supervisor should make sure that he undertakes the required activity for which he is responsible and which can be undertaken only by the supervisor. Those employed as supervisors by title of job function must face up to the fact that much of their effectiveness is diminished by clerical duties which should be undertaken by auxiliary personnel.

Guidelines for Evaluation. The supervisor's behavior as interpreted by the teacher and associated staff is of primary importance. Not only is a statemanship-like quality required when dealing with personnel, but also he must adhere to a pattern of commentary which will allow him to be effective regardless of with whom he comes in contact.

First. Commentary should be specific at all times. For many supervisors it takes an unwarranted amount of time to get to the point. Thus, a supervisor who has difficulty in expressing himself clearly with a minimum amount of verbiage needs to practice. When the supervisor does not come to the point of the discussion, the conference becomes awkward and is often an unpleasant experience for all concerned.

Second. Commentary should be comprehensive. A comprehensive statement can be made only when the conference and/or discussion concerns one or a limited number of topics. A supervisor should refrain from overgeneralizing, but he should speak about a given point or aspect of a discussion with complete coverage. A supervisor should refrain from definitive statements based upon limited available data.

Third. When engaging in a discussion informally, or at a scheduled conference, the supervisor should be sure that every one of his comments can be substantiated by documented data. Implications, rumor, misconceptions, and untruths have been the result of supervisory statements which have been basically those of bias, attitude, and inadequate information. Hearsay quoted by the supervisor is inexcusable; a supervisor is paid to know the facts of a given situation or have access to them upon request. Commentary should not be made by a supervisor unless it is based upon the known facts regardless of his personal professional position.

Fourth. A preplanned conference is essential, and it should be important enough not to be viewed as an incidental activity, "a thing to do," versus a part of the professional supervisory program. Again, supervisory attitude plays a key role in the success of a preplanned conference.

Fifth. The follow-up activities are the mortar of any program. Without follow-up activities which are of direct relevance to the instructional faculty, individually or collectively, the stigma of initiating without purpose will soon follow. Follow-up activities should be systematically carried out in close proximity in time to the evaluation conference. If a time lapse is allowed to intervene, the direct association with the conference and intended objective tends to be obscured.

Caution. The suggested guidelines focus upon those aspects which will assist a supervisor in having his program and teacher evaluation accepted. When evaluation can be interpreted as being helpful by nature of the assistance, a supervisor has a chance of having meaningful and continuous in-service follow-up activity within the educational objectives of the school system. Thus, a supervisor must know the instructional and associated personnel in terms of their strengths, weaknesses, strong feelings, biases, and professional positions. When effective teacher evaluation takes place, the supervisor deals with each situation in terms of the individual being counselled.

Appendix H

SUPERVISOR AND PERSONALIZATION OF INSTRUCTION

Attitude. Personalized instruction for children becomes a reality when the supervisor perceives instruction as being child centered versus teacher centered. At this point in time, many a teacher has the know-how and desire to work more on an individual basis with children only to be thwarted by a supervisor whose own background in professional knowledge has "gaps." Thus, personalization of instruction at all levels of learning, regardless of subject matter, hinges on the attitude of both the classroom teacher and the supervisor with respect to the pupil and classroom management.

Supervisory Responsibility. When accountability in the instructional setting is being emphasized, a supervisor has the responsibility to assist each classroom teacher in developing educational objectives which can be evaluated in terms of observable behavior. In effect, there is a need to develop criterion-based objectives which increase skill competencies for the learner.

Many a teacher may say that he has always had objectives but that he had not written them down. This may be true; however, the actual writing is the test of existing objectives. The form of the objective is not the question, but does it state the intent of instruction or independent learning activity and how it will be evaluated? The supervisor must assist the teacher to realize that children have and still do receive evaluation which has nothing to do with the task requested of them. Possibly a standard example is the child who incorrectly solves a story problem in arithmetic. Given the numbers to add, subtract, multiply, or divide, he may be able to solve the computation correctly; however, when the data is placed in a word-problem format, he is unable to arrive at the correct solution. The question is whether the evaluation is one of lacking in arithmetic knowledge or an inability to comprehend the written word. This type of evaluation can be isolated in other subject areas and at all levels of learning. Thus, there is a need for those who instruct to be increasingly more precise in their objectives and in stating how and to what level of acceptance a student must achieve.

In-service and Personalized Instruction. In-service sessions on the subject of personalizing/individualization of instruction have met with varying degrees of resistance all over the nation. As observers, the authors note that an undue stress is placed upon the writing of behavioral objectives in isolation of curriculum known to the teacher. Likewise, the levels of learning instructional domain remain unclear to the classroom teacher. Taxonomy presents another problem.

Simplifying the taxonomy categories to: knowledge, comprehension, application, and invention assists the teacher-writer to comprehend that much of his instruction heretofore and at the present is low level. Supervisors need to show teachers that the learner needs to become an ever-increasing independent learner with opportunities to apply his knowledge and to invent, as opposed to being a passive learner where facts and bits of miscellaneous knowledge dominate the act of learning. Thus, in-service workshops should provide a teacher with the specifics of personalized instruction and the encouragement to transfer it into the classroom setting at a rate the classroom teacher can professionally coordinate.

Appendix I

SELF-EVALUATION AND THE SUPERVISOR

Supervisor-Personality. When seeking to analyze self in the context of supervision, there is a tendency to examine the paper credentials and overlook the human qualities which are significant to supervisory success. Some consideration should be given to those persons who have had an evaluated internship within their professional background over those who have been teachers and have practiced the act of supervision on the job. This position is taken because a prospective supervisor should be evaluated in terms of supervisory skills, whereas the latter is known as an outstanding classroom teacher which does not guarantee effective supervisory competence.

When undertaking self-evaluation as a supervisor, the following questions should be considered:

1. Does the manner of the supervisor command respect?
2. Can he work within a framework which others have designed and which may not represent his total thinking?
3. When controversy is present, can the supervisor rise above the issue and coordinate as well as resolve the subject in question in an acceptable, professional way without injecting his own preferred position?
4. Does the supervisor perceive himself in a service role versus an authoritarian figure to dominate curriculum and in-service programming?
5. When counselling with a teacher, does the supervisor have genuine empathy for the situation as well as the person involved without becoming emotionally involved?

6. When problem-solving situations arise in the in-service setting or during a committee meeting, can the supervisor assume and maintain a guidance-function role and act as a resource person rather than a dominating influence?
7. Does the supervisor exercise an expertise role in all areas or does he call upon both faculty and outside consultants who are specialists?
8. When evaluating, does the supervisor restrict himself to judgments based upon documented data and refrain from stating superficial generalizations?
9. Can the supervisor work as a demonstration teacher without making the classroom teacher feel unworthy in teaching his own assigned students?
10. Does the supervisor accurately report his activity and that of the faculty to the administration in terms of established educational philosophy and school policy?

Humanism and the Supervisor. The supervisor has the most unique opportunity of any person in the educational enterprise to assist in effecting change. Those who aspire to such a position must welcome variety, controversy, continual problem-solving, constant evaluation, and modification. Above all, he must represent the best of mankind who seeks to serve and perceive his success to be in the realm of assisting professional personnel to help themselves in the creation of a more purposeful curriculum at the local school level.

Glossary

GLOSSARY

Academic license. Academic license is that attitude espoused by some who instruct, that they may undertake to study in class whatsoever may be of interest to the instructor and/or his pupils without any concern for course objectives.

Accountable. Accountable refers to the act of showing that intended objectives have been fulfilled based upon the application of analyzed data.

Administration. Administration is a process composed of personnel who are responsible for the development, initiation, maintenance, and evaluation of curriculum development and physical facilities.

Administrative function. Administrative function refers to a component part of the activities of administration.

Analyst. An analyst is one who carefully plans his supervisory program and systematically carries it out in terms of stated instructional objectives.

Attitude of professional service. Attitude of professional service refers to that observable behavior of an educator who consistently exhibits concern for the learning process first and ambition second, regardless of his present assignment. A function of self-discipline.

Authority-centered. Authority-centered refers to a person ". . . who sees established authority, absolute principles, expert opinion, and common practices as the 'right' answer to problems . . ."

Bright and gifted. The term "bright and gifted" is associated with those students who demonstrate an exceptional basic knowledge in an area of study both academic and applied.

Consensus. A consensus refers to common opinion, thinking, and a judgment expressed within a select group of persons.

Course of study. Course of study is a designed sequence of learning experiences relative to a selected content field.

Criterion performance objective. Criterion performance objectives are those initial, intermediate, or terminal competencies which include: (1) the given data for the learner to use, (2) a statement of performance, and (3) on what level the learner must perform for it to be acceptable.

Curriculum development. Curriculum development is the sequence of activities and personnel involvement required to design a course of study.

Curriculum specialist. Curriculum specialist is that person who specializes in curriculum design to meet predetermined behavioral objectives.

Cybernetics. Cybernetics is derived from the Greek word (kybernētēs) meaning "steerman." Feedback principle is fundamental to this system of analysis.

Demonstration teacher. A demonstration teacher is one who is able to successfully instruct children with selected method and technique in such a manner that the teachers who are observing can comprehend intended instructional outcomes as well as be able to teach in a similar manner with their own assigned classroom of children.

Dysfunction. Dysfunctions are those sets of factors or problems which serve to limit or prevent problem resolution.

Enrichment. Enrichment refers to those instructional activities both teacher guided and individually directed which provide horizontal knowledge to supplement what is already known. Enrichment should not be associated with additional assignments.

Evaluation. Evaluation is a continuous process which utilizes informal and formal measurement instruments for the purpose of making judgments concerning the accomplishment of educational objectives.

Evaluation instruments. Evaluation instruments refer to those predesigned instruments which measure to what extent an initial, intermediate, or terminal objective has been achieved.

Evaluative procedures. Evaluative procedures are those formats and informal instruments used by the supervisor to gather and analyze data to determine the success of a planned supervisory program.

Extra-legal force. Extra-legal force is a person (or persons) representing a special interest and exerting pressure to influence policy decisions which may be at variance with professional analysts.

Facilitating the learning process. Facilitating the learning process refers to the marshalling of personnel, physical plant, and instructional resources for the expressed purpose of curriculum implementation.

Feedback. Feedback is a reciprocal action where the first activity causes a second to take place, which in turn modifies the first activity.

Flexibility. Flexibility is a facet of the supervisory personality which perceives more than one approach to any given instructional problem.

Follow-up. Follow-up is the systematic examination of ongoing activities for the purpose of modification.

Follow-up activities. Follow-up activities are those prescribed to assist the classroom teacher after problem and analysis are discussed in decision-making.

Function. Function is the act of doing.

Hidden agenda. Hidden agenda is an ulterior motive usually kept a secret until such time as it will effect maximum influence in decision-making.

Individual centered. Individual centered refers to that person who ". . . sees the most desirable behavior as that which most closely approximates the judgment of those who are or will be performing a particular task."

Initiation syndrome. Initiation syndrome refers to educational leadership that is idea oriented by the capacity to manage those local factors which create a climate conducive to change.

Inner directed. Inner directed refers to a person who ". . . sees the most desirable behavior as that which most closely approximates the judgment of those who are or will be performing a particular task."

In-service education. In-service education is the professional study and work by the faculty and staff to improve the existing curricula or design new curricula.

Instructional function. Instructional function is the act of teaching.

Instructional problem. An instructional problem is any aspect of the educational enterprise under analysis for the purpose of modification.

Instructional specialist. Instructional specialist is that person who demonstrates teaching expertise in a given content field.

Keeping school. Keeping school refers to the leadership behavior exercised at the neighborhood school or public/private school system level that functions within the legal statutes without benefit of an educational philosophy and/or coordinated educational sequences based upon criterion performance objectives.

Lateral transmission. Lateral transmission is the sharing of knowledge by the informed with the uninformed regardless of age or academic preparation.

Leadership. Leadership refers to the act of creating confidence in others and guiding relevant activities toward predetermined educational objectives.

Management expertise. Management expertise is the ability to successfully coordinate activities of the supervisory function.

Manipulation. Manipulation is the deliberate act of unscrupulous persuasion of self-centered reasons.

Measurement. Measurement refers to instruments commercially or individually designed to ascertain data on a specific subject.

Modification. Modification is the change made within an initiated program and/or project to obtain the intended terminal objectives.

Other centered. Other centered refers to that person who ". . . sees his ability to reflect accurately the wishes of others as the crux of his leadership."

Pedestrian trivia. Pedestrian trivia refers to the inconsequential activities carried out by administrators which could be undertaken by less credentialed personnel. Some of these activities are counting lunch money and dispersing materials.

Phase-in. Phase-in is the result of focus and designated priority whereby rate of implementation is established for the purpose of assuring a higher level of success.

Planning. Planning is the systematic order whereby a given set of instructional tasks are formulated and ranked by priority.

Predictor. A predictor is one who supervises infrequently and relies on anticipated outcomes versus an objective analysis of gathered data.

Procedure. Procedure is an orderly sequence within process.

Remedial instruction. Remedial instruction refers to that instruction which is designed to improve the level of learning of an individual who has been diagnosed as being deficient in skills which other children of the same age normally have mastered.

Research. Research refers to both library and action study where programs are carefully subjected to controls for evaluation.

Residual consequences. Residual consequences are the natural levels to which professional activities sink when evaluated unworthy or less than meaningful for participation by the instructional specialist.

Rigidity. Rigidity is characteristic of supervisory behavior which perceives only one way of solving an instructional problem.

Service function. Service function refers to the professional intent of supervisory activities.

Significant others. Significant others are those non-school personnel who have the authority to exert influence upon school policy.

Statesmanship. Statesmanship is the capacity of an individual to coordinate divergent points of view and weld them into a purposeful accord which serves to carry out the philosophy of education, designated priorities, and long-range plans at any level of supervisory-administrative responsibility.

Supervision. Supervision is the coordinated direction of instructional leadership and evaluation within the public and private schools.

Supervisor. Supervisor is a person who specializes in curriculum design and implementation.

Supervisory function. Supervisory function is the means by which a supervisor carries out his planned activities.

Supervisory guidance function. Supervisory guidance function is that facet of supervisory behavior which analyzes participant contribution and coordinates it so as to bring about the best possible solution in terms of participant input.

Supervisory personality. Supervisory personality is the interpreted behavior of a supervisor by the administration and instructional personnel.

Taxonomy. Taxonomy refers to the classification of instruction into levels of outcomes: (1) knowledge, (2) comprehension, (3) application, and (4) invention.

Technique. Technique is the method or details of procedure.

Tenured syndrome. Tenured syndrome is a condition of both faculty and administration which over time affects their professional behavior and subsequently their sensitivity to accountability which may go so far as to exercise unwarranted prerogatives and instructional license.

Theory. Theory is an approximation resulting from an analysis of organized data.

Work group oriented. Work group oriented refers to a person who ". . . tries to help the people concerned or involved

in the program to identify their own purposes with
those of the school program."

Enrichment Readings

CHANGING BUSINESS VALUES

Ted R. Brannen

University of Houston
Houston, Texas

The task of schools of business administration is to prepare much of the nation's young leadership for future positions in the decision process. To succeed in this task, we educators must have some notion of the type of world in which our students will be asked to assume responsibility. We need to anticipate the purposes they will serve, the goals of change toward which they will exert their influence, the knowledge they will need, and the techniques they will require for the analyses and decisions they will face.

We expect our students to be involved in the process of selecting goals and purposes for themselves, for the organizations that employ them, and for society as a whole. Selections from among alternative goals involve human values. They will need the sensitivity to recognize alternative value opportunities, the courage to choose among competing values, and the ability to justify (at least to themselves) the value judgements they make.

For two hundred years there has been general agreement on the primary goal of our way of life. In the briefest terms, that goal has been economic growth and security. The efforts that have been organized by that goal have produced the most glorious Golden Age in the history of man. Our so-

---

Reprinted by permission from Business Education Forum, Vol. 25 (May, 1971), pp. 31-33.

ciety achieved more progress in these years than was achieved in the previous 100,000 years of man's existence.

In a single lifetime, man has advanced his science and technology from travel by horse and buggy to interplanetary rockets, from "bleeding" as a medical remedy to organ transplants, from the telegraph to worldwide transmission of images via satellites, from steam to nuclear power, and from computation by paper and pencil to large electronic computors. During this lifetime man has learned to travel 2,000 times faster, compute millions of times faster, and repair himself from a growing inventory of human spare parts.

We have progressed a great distance toward the affluence that has been our goal. But now we are discovering the age of affluence is less than totally satisfying. We are keenly aware that our streets and homes are not safe. Weapons of total destruction have become available before men have found means other than armed conflict to settle their differences. The organization of society is too tenuous, in fact, to resolve even such controversies as an appropriate length for hair or skirts.

Dissatisfaction with our way of life is resulting in criticisms from several directions. New power blocs are emerging in efforts to force changes in the established system. The youth revolt, consumerism, and militant minority movements are bringing many of our old values and methods under attack. These criticisms and attacks on the established order are leading to the separation of society along a scale of divisiveness. At one extreme of this scale are groups which argue for the preservations of the established order without fundamental change. At the other extreme are groups which advocate the destruction of our traditional way of life followed by a period of rebuilding from the ashes. In between these extremes are other groups favoring various types of reform.

The supporters of the established way of life argue that changes in our traditional values would jeopardize the continued availability of the enlarged flow of goods, accumulated wealth, and expanded leisure those values have produced. They hold that the good life now enjoyed by most members of industrialized societies is attributed to the motivation, efficiency, and economic justice provided by automatic market forces, a competitive environment, and individual acquisitiveness. They believe the quest for individual gain organizes people and induces them to conform to positions and activities that have been planned to produce efficiency. They believe that only by rewarding competitive superiority can society protect individual freedom, provide jobs with satisfactory wages, assure profits, and motivate individuals to high degrees of commitment. They accept the level of profits or the Gross National Product as being the closest measure of society's success in achieving the good life. Moreover, they maintain that the traditional values will continue to produce more wealth and, hence, an improved way of life in the future.

The critics of the established way of life, on the other hand, are dissatisfied with the order of our priorities, regimentation of individuals by large institutions and generalized standards, business as a way of life, militarization of our society, economic oppression and artificial scarcities, racism, hypocrisy, irrelevance in education, dishonesty in advertising, inaccuracy in communications media, impersonality in American life, and overreaction to partially self-induced fears of other ways of life. There are specific complaints about price fixing, automotive and pharmaceutical safety, products of negative or spurious value, pollution, the prodigal use of resources, bureaucratic disregard for individual needs, and immorality in international relations.

Thus one side of the controversy argues that it is unwilling to give up the progress that has solved many of the problems of poverty man has faced, and the other side argues that the new problems associated with that progress are too dear a price to pay. Yet the critics seem to have serious difficulty in expressing what they offer as a substitute for the established way of life. They do not suggest alternative ways of motivating individuals to contribute to the ongoing productive process that is responsible for the age of affluence. They criticize the work ethic and the emphasis on profit motivation of the past, but they speak only vaguely of humanist values as substitutes. They sometimes retreat to the position that the answer must be a return to an earlier way of life. The difficulty here is that the earlier way of life did not provide advanced health care, comfort, or research to expose the secrets of the atom and the universe.

When members of a society share a common goal they can cooperate in organized productive effort. There does not seem to be an inconsistency between individual autonomy and social control. Individuality and self-determination seem to be supported by mutual constraints and organized endeavor. Conflicts that arise can be resolved by achieving agreement of the nature of the problem and reaching some trade-off or compromise. Controversies, under these conditions, are likely to be beneficial because they mobilize interests, cause reconsideration of old ideas, induce needed revisions in thoughts and actions, and stimulate improved approaches to new and old problems.

But conflict that is not supported by goal coherence may lead to tactics that immobilize an entire society. Organization can be maintained only by some form of coercion. This may cause destructive conflict because enforced conformity to the requirements of organized endeavor may be viewed by individuals as oppressive and stultifying, even immoral. Competition among ideas is desirable, but there needs to be a basis for deriving some satisfactory resolution of the controversy.

We seem to lack a basis for resolving the conflict that now rages in our streets, on our campuses, and in our families. The current mood is more one of growing intolerance than one of search for means of resolving the issues. This growing hostility indicates we have lost the general acceptance for the primary goal of economic growth that previously existed. Thus the conflict is becoming dangerous. The stability of our society is threatened. We must endeavor to regain the order and organization that produced the rapid progress of recent decades. We may continue to progress toward solutions to problems of pollution and interpersonal relations without retaining the earlier goal of economic expansion, but we cannot continue to progress without order and organization.

This indicates a critical need for a basis from which to develop mutual interests and cooperation among the conflicting groups in our society. Out of the criticisms and conflicts that are centered around our traditional way of life must come a new direction, a new national goal, a new purpose for life.

Fortunately, we seem to be witnessing the emergence of a new goal that may gain general acceptance and that may offer a basis for resolving the conflicts that are endangering our way of life. The goal of an expanding Gross National Product appears to be undergoing an important revision as a result of the criticisms leveled against it. The organizing philosophy of our total society may change from economic security to ecological security.

We should understand that a change in the organizing goal of our way of life from economic security to ecological security has widespread ramifications. It portends a change in many of the basic values of our society. Changes in our values will affect our requirements and objectives. This means the decision criteria and the measures of effectiveness we employ will also need to be revised.

Individual competitive acquisitiveness may cease to be the embodiment of the ideal values of our society. Individual wealth achieved through applications of the old pattern of values may be seen to be contributory to problems of pollution, racism, immorality, and suppression of the individualism of others.

Simplistic profit and loss statements may no longer

provide an adequate basis for decisions. A comparison of costs, revenues, and return on capital that would have signaled a legitimate project in the past may not justify that same project in the future. A marketing program that would produce a satisfactory dollar return may be rejected for reasons of esthetics, traffic congestion, or employee hardship.

If such a change occurs in the organizing philosophy of our society, it will not be easy to make the necessary adjustments in our thinking and our problem analyses. We may have to recognize that contemporary technology is creating a world in which individuals are becoming so interdependent that improvement in the quality of life must be sought for all men or for none. We will have to train ourselves to look beyond immediate decisions and to conceptualize many of the secondary consequences that will spread out from the point of impact to influence many other activities, relationships, and problems. This will necessitate new and expanded techniques of analysis. We will need to apply the concepts of social accounting that are beginning to emerge. Finance and marketing decisions will have to be evaluated in terms of their probable impact on our chances for survival. The improving techniques of management information systems will be needed to strengthen our ability to quantify and process data. The applied behavioral sciences will need to be used more extensively to determine our needs and guide the development of decision criteria. Moreover, all of these areas of knowledge will need to be used together in a process of discipline synthesis rather than independently by discipline specialists.

The search for truth is made difficult by the fact that our perceptions are influenced not only by the facts but also by the frames of reference from which we view the facts. A most important determinant of our frames of reference is the pattern of values we have deposited in the latent structure that underlies our cognitive and affective responses to experience. Frequently we are unaware of our own value structures. We have merely learned to view good and bad in certain ways without consciously evaluating the alternative concepts of right and wrong that we might have adopted.

Sensitivity training groups, or T-groups, are some success in helping individuals see themselves as others see them. We need to help our students surface their values and look at them with a similar candor. Each person needs to probe his own beliefs, prejudices, and assumptions regarding the nature of good and bad and the ideal world he is endeavoring to help create.

Of course, faculty members who approach the problem of value judgements may encounter opposition. Many people resist and resent questions regarding their values. Traditional centers of power in society may feel threatened by value probes that could lead to changes in the status quo. Too often the role of business schools has been defined to include the indoctrination of students on the validity or importance of established values. Should we risk playing a role in a situation that is sure to generate conflict between some who are seeking truth and some who are seeking to protect and perpetuate the comfortable ideas and values of the past? I believe we cannot avoid playing a role in this situation if we are seriously concerned about effective communication. Our goal must be to seek understanding, not indoctrination.

SUNBEAMS OUT OF CUCUMBERS: WHY AND HOW TRAINING FOR LEADERSHIP IN EDUCATION MUST CHANGE[1]

Marcella Brenner

Professor of Education
George Washington University
Washington, D. C.

> He had been eight years upon a project for extracting sunbeams out of cucumbers, which were to be put in phials hermetically sealed, and let out to warm the air in inclement summers.
>
> --Gulliver's Travels, Part III, Chapter V, "Voyage to Laputa."

Present training programs for principals and supervisors are absurdly irrelevant. Advisors help candidates plan a series of courses, with the assumption that by some process of magic they will lead to competence in leadership. But the courses are not magical, nor do they produce competence any more than Swift's cucumbers produced sunbeams.

Practically all school systems need a new kind of leadership; yet, those that need it most are blind to its value. Despite a recognitized urgency for change and expenditures of large sums of money, efforts by school systems are doomed

---

Reprinted by permission from Journal of Teacher Education, Vol. 22 (Winter, 1971), pp. 434-442.

1. The author would like to acknowledge the valuable criticism and editorial assistance given by Pauline M. Shereshifsky and Joyce Sartwell.

to failure unless they can create a strong group of middle-level leaders. No school superintendent, no matter how flexible, open, and secure, can bring necessary change to a school system without competent administrators; yet it is a rare principal who has been adequately trained for his job.

The Administrative Tradition

What teacher eager for status, chafing under his principal, and needing more money does not leap at the chance to become principal himself? However, once in the job, he often finds it demanding beyond reason; but fearful of a poor rating, he dares not reveal his inadequacy to his superiors. He is not even supposed to need help, for there is clearly no provision for it in the school system or in the university that labeled him administrator by virtue of his master's degree. Consequently, once a successful teacher becomes a fretful, frustrated, ineffective principal, chiefly because his training for the principalship consisted of a flat, stale package of traditional master's degree courses, his experience with other adults during his teaching career was minimal in a professional sense; and most crucially of all, his opportunity to develop the supportive skills in working with adults (so necessary to a principal's effectiveness) was practically nonexistent.

In order to create a body of effective leadership, there must be an upheavaling of present leadership training programs. We must move from the assumption that superior classroom teaching experience, plus covering course work, will in itself prepare anyone adequately for principalship or supervision. Preparation that involves only teaching effectiveness and/or the traditional descriptive approach to school administration and finance is clearly inadequate in the light of the complexities of educational leadership today. Even administrative internships, where they presently exist, have built-in failure strategies. There is no assurance that a trainee will gain the insights and competence he needs just because he is placed in a school office as acting vice-principal and assigned tasks for which he has no ultimate responsibility. True, he may learn a few tricks and coping maneuvers, but he cannot be expected to obtain professional insights that will be useful to him and applicable to other situations, particularly if he is working under someone who is ill-trained himself. To express this more positively, professional growth is much more likely to occur when the trainee is actively working in a leadership role, while at the same time receiving supportive professional mentorship. Though some school systems have so-called training programs in which interns are assigned to administrative posts and meet monthly with a top member of the system, this is not likely to work effectively, for the simple reason that the mentor is an in-house person who, in the intern's eyes, is not to be trusted. The trainee can relax more quickly with an outsider who is not associated with any of the power centers of a school system. It can be altogether too hazardous to expose one's limitations, or even one's strengths, to a member of the hierarchy.

The Problem

The purpose of this article is to persuade those of us who have the power to make change that we must stop the traditional nontraining of administrators and develop training programs that will make some sense in the light of today's demands for leaders and the trainees' readiness to meet them. Developing authentic leaders in education is a formidable task, in which both the colleges and the schools must join efforts and resources. We must be more sophisticated about the nature of change and growth. We can no longer afford the naive assumption that the possession of a master's degree indicates leadership potential, much less competence. Nor can we continue to expect that realistic leadership training will be expensive. It will be costly in dollars, and state and local monies will be needed. But what we are doing now--or not doing--is even more expensive in terms of both financial and human resources.

A New Kind of Leadership Training Program

The leadership training program at George Washington University is an attempt to provide a catalytic force in transforming teachers into competent leaders who can work confidently in an atmosphere of change. Its major thrust is a closely supervised practicum in which candidates on leave for a full semester have live field experiences in the real school and community and at the same time receive active supervision and support.

The program also attempts to challenge present ideas of leadership training at two levels: (1) by providing an example to schools of education throughout the country to adopt a practicum as part of the professional training for administrators and supervisors and (2) by encouraging school systems to give active support to teachers who seek this type of practical professional training. Ideally, this support should take the form of leave with pay; that is, fully subsidized, full-time freedom to study and learn. Heretofore, the approach of school systems has been to expect teachers to get their graduate degrees by attending classes in the evenings, on Saturday mornings, and during summer sessions. Such an approach has only contributed to the practice of getting credits rather than acquiring increased skills with which to attack pressing social and psychological problems.

In February 1967, ten teachers from five nearby school systems in the District of Columbia; Montgomery and Prince Georges Counties, Maryland; and Fairfax and Arlington[2] Counties, Virginia, met to begin their leadership training

---

2. Arlington County support and commitment helped to initiate the program.

under the new G. W. program, the many facets of which are described below. All ten, who had been recommended by their school systems as persons destined for leadership roles, had been given full tuition grants by the University and sabbatical or professional full-time leave from their classrooms from February to June, during which they would work at the practicum as well as take several courses leading eventually to the necessary master's degree in administration.

Although the neighboring school system endorsed the plan, they had no administrative devices for freeing teachers for half a year nor the money to support it, so of necessity only those who could afford reduced pay could participate in the program.[3] In the first year, all were women; in the second year, there were two men; in the third, one; and in the fourth, two. The total group met regularly every Wednesday morning from 9 to 12; at other times, they met in smaller groups or individually for counseling.

Facing the Unknown

It should be immediately clear that the G. W. leadership training program is just a beginning, and in no sense a total change in the stance of the college with regard to the demands of leadership. An examination of colleges' catalogues shows little, if any, change in the last twenty years in the requirements for a master's degree in education. Nor is there anywhere else any evidence of an attempt to offer an integrated program based on supervised problem solving in actual live experiences.

Understandably, then, it was difficult for the fellows, as they were called, to believe that this leadership train-

3. Financed assistance from the University, the Washington Project, and the Eugene and Agnes E. Meyer Foundation provided stipends, plus tuition, in 1970 and 1971.

ing program would be any different. The most skeptical were the more experienced, veterans of years of double-talk, whose teachers' workshops had been distinguished more by advance notices than by worthwhile activities. Many tried to conceal their doubts, but their anxiety was manifested in a score of ways: How many books are required? What about a final exam? No term papers? You mean you really want me to decide what I want to do? Where's the catch? Of course, no amount of explaining was at this point reassuring. It took weeks (and for some, even months) before they believed they were free, even expected, to question, to pursue their own interests, to think. A few remained wary all through the semester.

In the beginning, some of the fellows required many hours of counseling with the instructor of the psychiatric consultant, Dr. E. James Lieberman,[4] in order to get on their feet emotionally. Some had great difficulty in separating themselves from their former classrooms and children. It was more comfortable to look backward to a situation where they were marked as a superior than to look forward into uncertainty and challenge. They found it hard to be on their own, freed from the regimen of 9 to 4. Later in the program, their supervision of beginning teachers caused other kinds of anxiety. Support during these periods was crucial.

<u>The Practicum</u>. The fellows learned that the practicum would include tasks in schools with teachers, parents, and community leaders that would make the same kinds of demands upon them as are made upon any other principal or supervisor. Central to the practicum would be their opportunity to su-

---

4. Dr. Lieberman is not a psychiatrist searching for pathology, but a man clinically trained and community-orientated, who helped us in a process that is based on normal functioning. His kind of psychiatric counsel makes possible the exploration of areas of personality and the development of leadership qualities.

pervise one or more beginning teachers under the guidance of a University mentor, who would be there to help them through their anxieties, ambivalence, and uncertainty about how they might best support the beginning teacher. In addition to trying to understand the dynamics of interpersonal relationships, the fellow found he would spend much time on leadership and supervisory techniques, locating professional resources, uncovering local community problems, and reading current professional and related literature.

The Seminar. The first seminars centered on specific educational ideas or books, but the subjects discussed during the early weeks did not require a great deal of background knowledge on the part of the fellows. The object was not only to share information but to introduce to the fellows an attitude and approach toward it that would grow and be nourished by them all. Accordingly, there was much dialogue: talk in close relationship with one another, talk that acknowledged each person's experience of joy and travail, talk punctured by frequent asides and interruptions. It was believed that this kind of discourse was one way to ensure that the student of the professional learned to experience his experiences.

. . . .

The seminar began with reading and discussing current books, such as Peter Schrag's Voices in the Classroom or a classic like Bowlby's Child Care and the Growth of Love, or a chapter from Jersild or Redl. The group was encouraged to be free, open, and questioning. It was not without difficulty and some pain that the teachers were persuaded to speak freely; to disagree without elaborate apology; and hardest of all, to admit without rationalization that they were ill-informed about a man, a technique, or an idea.

Some of the early seminars, often led by experts on the

subject, dealt with communication skills, interview techniques, and current problems in local elementary schools. Later, one fellow wrote:

> It was during these meetings that I gathered a measure of confidence in my own abilities, overcoming an initial uncertainty. My communication skills, I feel, grew as I became involved in the discussions and less self-conscious about how I sounded.

Another wrote: "Never before have I had to think so hard."

Field Work Experiences. It was important that the fellows get started on their individual programs as soon as possible. Their field work would give them immediate opportunities to test their newly acquired insights, and subsequent Wednesday mornings would be open for clarification and refinement of shared experiences. The role of the instructor was that of facilitator, making suggestions and arrangements.

> Supervising the new teacher. Each of the ten would now begin to supervise at least one beginning teacher. To the University staff, this appeared to be quite feasible since their MAT students, who are placed in jobs in February, had replaced some of the ten in their classrooms. On second thought, however, it was decided that it would not be wise for the fellows to try to supervise their replacements. It is too difficult for the children, the intern, and the fellow to cope with the problems of separation and mixed loyalty inevitable in such an arrangement.
>
> Supervising the interns was a task the fellows were eager to try. As capable teachers with many years of experience, they felt thoroughly able to be helpful. Their biggest problem was the dismay they experienced when the beginning teacher did not immediately respond, when they had to accept and understand refusal or rejection. It is difficult to face rebuff, and even more difficult to accept the fact that it is the learner who has the power to decide what and when he will learn. Although the supervisor takes care to pay attention to the many-faceted nature of the

learning going on within the intern, he cannot be solely responsible for the outcome. Such a philosophy necessitates tolerance for the performance of the inexperienced and ability to help the teacher slowly, to stand by while he gradually increases his knowledge and skill.

Essential to the fellow's role as supervisor was his understanding that the intern needed more than anything else a sense of the fellow's strength and a realization that the fellow recognized in him a strength of his own. If a supervisor offers criticism in such a way that the teacher is an active participant (has his own acknowledged), he is allowing that teacher to use the criticism as a means of helping himself. But when he offers criticism so that he alone is active in giving the criticism and the teacher is passive as the recipient, the only activity left to the teacher is resistance.

Principals and supervisors tend to relax demands when young teachers are having trouble. Out of sympathy for the teacher who is clearly tired, discouraged, and afraid that he will fail, they are willing to overlook too frequent absences, dirty blackboards, books in disarray, and poor planning. The new teacher doesn't particularly love the kids at this point either because, as he sees it, they are making him fail. And yet this is precisely where the neophyte must be required to meet the high standards expected of him in his job. T. N. Berlin expresses this very well:

> The more troubled and anxious a teacher is in his work, the more important it is that he be helped to do his job better. One way of working toward better teaching performance is to set high standards for every aspect of the job. Tardiness, slovenliness, and inaccuracy, if overlooked, lead to ever increasing difficulties, accompanied by increasing anxiety about holding the position. Thus, the more troubled the teacher, the attentive the administrator must be to details. The administrator's constant insistence on better performance and willingness to accept the teacher's anger without retaliation eventually result in a better job and increased pleasure in teaching. . . . I am aware that in every teachers college there are a few professors, supervisors, and seminar leaders who explore the subject of teachers' feelings. I also know administrators

> who help their teachers immeasurably by blending firmness and sympathetic understanding. It is my hope . . . that more and more teachers will be able to count on the support that the right blend of understanding and firmness in an administrator can bring a school staff.[5]

What about rating teachers? It was suggested to the fellows that once they had achieved the status of administrators they begin the year with allowing teachers to set up their own criteria for evaluation. Once these criteria are established, the teacher is entitled to competent criticism; his use of it becomes his way of helping himself. The supervisor and teacher together define the need for change: it is essential to be specific and identify the alternatives. After this initial evaluation, the administrator needs to encourage frequent dialogue. The teacher knows what problems he is working on and can listen to criticism without feeling that he is being attacked.

In working with the beginning teachers, the fellows also had an opportunity to deal with most of the other components of the supervisory situation. They learned the importance of careful intervention strategies. They acquired the techniques of clearing with all levels of the hierarchy in a school system. They learned the importance of making endless copies of all--even the most harmless--communications, so that the principal, the supervisor, the area director, and the central office were kept informed. They became aware of how powerful are secretaries, how busy and defensive are principals, and how suspicious are supervisors.

Some of the fellows asked for a supervisory experience in districts other than their own. Thus, there was a District of Columbia fellow supervising in Montgomery and Prince Georges Counties, and Virginia people supervising in the District of Montgomery County. The fellows had to develop rapport with the principal of the school in which the intern was teaching, the local supervisor, and the grade chairman, as well as with the young beginning teacher.

---

5. I. N. Berlin. "Teachers' Self-Expectations: How Realistic Are They?" <u>The School Review</u>, Vol. 66 (Summer, 1958), pp. 134-143.

The Wednesday practicum provided the necessary shelter. It was a safe place in which to talk over problems in an effort to increase insights into the helping process and themselves as helpers.

Acknowledging individual interests. One vital way to arrive at leadership competence is to acknowledge the importance of each person's individual interests. In addition to supervising a new teacher, each fellow was given a series of field placements in which his individual interests were considered. Most wanted to shadow principals in large, small, urban, and rural schools; two made extensive use of videotape as a tool in teacher education; some paired up with general supervisors; one D. C. fellow was assigned to sit with the Arlington, Virginia, supervising staff.

All of the first (1967) group of fellows attended the annual meeting of the American Orthopsychiatric Association, held in the District of Columbia. The second year of the leadership training program, a small out-of-pocket fund was available, which made possible a trip to New York City to see an experimental reading program, the talking typewriter, and the Guggenheim Museum. The fellows also attended the annual meeting of the Association for Supervision and Curriculum Development, considered a high point by the group, in Atlantic City. In other years, they attended a reading conference in Philadelphia, an American Association of School Administrators convention in Atlantic City, the National Conference for Teachers of English in St. Louis, and visited the American Association of Elementary-Kindergarten-Nursery Educators in Washington, D. C.

Reading Program. In addition to working out in the field, each fellow organized his own reading program as he became aware of his needs. One found he needed to familiarize himself with current thinking about the new math and the use of differentiated staffing. Another needed to read about the open classroom and the Leicestershire plan; a third, about English as a second language. A good part of the reading consisted of learning very basic concepts in education and allied fields. All of the fellows needed to backtrack to material they should have learned as teachers before they could move forward toward learning what they needed to know as administrators. Once a fellow had immersed himself in this background material, he could devote seminar time to the more difficult part: finding out what he thought about basic concepts and new ideas, and why.

For years, it has been a truism in this country that to be a teacher is to be a paragon of moral conduct. All of our fellows were fresh from teaching, where they had been expected to conform; to be reliable, responsible, hardworking, prompt; and generally, to possess all the virtues and restraints of the classic Victorian governess. Thus the fellow had not come to see himself as one whose opinions should be sought. As a result, he had never learned to consider a new--or even old--idea in a genuinely professional and responsible fashion, with confidence that he could rely on his own judgement. It made many of the fellows uncomfortable to view themselves as leaders who henceforth would have to take hold of implications and make judgements. Most important of all was their sudden, disturbing realization that a passive or non-judgemental posture on their part would actually be a form of judgement for which they were responsible.

Increasing Professional Understanding of Behavior. Teachers-in-training--and the fellows were no exception--rarely get enough training designed to give them a theoretical understanding of behavior. All that most states require is a single course in psychology, usually psychology of learning, in which the student is expected to spend roughly thirty hours. No state requires its teachers to have had any work in mental health:[6] many schools of education do not offer such courses. The dynamics of group behavior receives even less attention, if possible.

---

6. Elizabeth H. Woellner and M. Autrilla Wood. Requirements for Certification of Teachers, Counselors, Librarians, Administrators for Secondary Schools, Junior Colleges, 34th ed. Chicago: University of Chicago Press, 1969.

Consequently, with some noteworthy exceptions, all the fellows had need of a greater understanding of normal behavior, their own and that of others, as well as some professional sophistication about how to use community resources or how to go about seeking professional help for a child or family. Many had had in their classes children who had been given a psychological evaluation, yet some had never had a conference with a psychologist whether to get or to give information; some had never talked with a psychiatrist and indeed didn't even know the difference between a psychiatrist and a psychologist; others had never read, except in textbooks, a psychologist's or social worker's report on a child or family. Although this may sound incredible, written as it is about superior teachers from five different school systems in a large metropolitan area, it is nevertheless not only true but common.

Much class time, therefore, went into a consideration of what should already have been understood: for example, how to help parents understand a seven-year-old who suddenly exhibits signs of infantile regression; how to cope with children who are aggressive, who don't seem to care, or who care too much. Throughout the discussions, an attempt was made to reach into the meaning of behavior as well as its causes. The administrator must deal with the child's or adult's behavior here and now; learning the meaning of behavior is one key to a successful solution of problems.

How to deal with unearned hostility, particularly from parents, took a great deal of working through. This problem pointed up the necessity for the fellow to develop a professional posture. By this is meant learning to use the relationship with the angry parent in solving the child's (or perhaps the teacher's or parent's) problem. An effort was made to help each fellow avoid the easy way out; approaching a parent Dale Carnegie-fashion with mollifying, pacifying, or charming attitude that refuses to acknowledge honestly the parent or his anger. The professional responsibility to so far more than just cope is frightening to the fledgling administrator. The repercussions either in the family, the community, or the superintendent's office of ineptly handled parent conferences can produce an ever widening area of dissatisfaction; on the other hand, a conference well handled can produce a dramatic change for good in a child and incalculable community support for the school.

To produce an affirmative parent conference--one that will be useful to the child, the parent, and the school--administrators must learn interview skills and be able to teach them to their teachers; or by example and encouragement, create a willingness in teachers to learn such skills. They should also want to dig below the surface. All too often an inarticulate parent hides his better qualities--warmth, understanding--until they are drawn out by the partner in the interview. But interview skills, willingness to penetrate beneath the surface, even love and affection, are not enough. In the end, the parent will interpret the interview in the light of its result, which depends on the competence of the administrator and the effort he puts into getting for the child and/or parent what he really needs.

Developing a Professional Self. In the practicum, an attempt was made to create authentic relationships the future administrator could use, to replace sterile lists of recommended procedures and practices with an honest understanding of relationships upon which the future administrator could build his professional skills. It was felt that a person develops leadership ability as he learns to use himself well in relation to others. How was this relationship provided in the practicum? By creating the supportive kind of environment in which each fellow could learn to be unafraid of expressing his needs, doubts, and insights. This support seemed to be one of the most essential aspects of the practicum, creating a flow between and among the participants --from mentor to fellow, from fellow to fellow, and from fellow to mentor.

Carl Rogers has suggested that it is the way a client's attitudes are perceived that makes a difference to the client, and it is this perception that is crucial. It seemed that as each candidate saw himself empathizing with others he came to believe that at least some, if not all, of the others were accepting and endorsing him. A major goal was to free the fellows to look at their feelings and share them. One device was the writing of a life history by each one, from which he read selected passages aloud to the class.[7] It was clear from these readings that many of the fellows, although struggling to be open, were still unable to acknowledge anger, hostility, fear, prejudice, and stereotypical attitudes. Desire for status and personal ambition were equally hard to acknowledge. A few of the fellows, after struggling with their professional selves throughout the practicum, realized that they did not want to work with adults at all.

The transition from awareness of self to the development of a professional self is a continuous process of growth, perception, and integration of learning. Some of the fellows' problems demonstrated two of the goals all were working toward: (a) to be able to be spontaneous and honest in their reactions, while disciplining those reactions in the service of another; (b) to develop sufficient knowledge of subject matter and theory to be able to be helpful, not just palliative, toward kids, teachers, and parents in trouble.

For some of the fellows, change was not necessary. They came with fine minds, well-developed skills, and excellent ideas. They did not need to change but merely to be confirmed in their goals and refreshed in spirit. Some were simply intellectually and professionally lonely; they flourished with the opportunity to join a small community of thoughtful persons.

Evaluation

This year, it was possible to offer Dr. Lieberman's

---

7. Use of autobiographical fragments was suggested by Dr. Gardner Murphy.

help to the former fellows of the leadership training program who are now in their new administrative positions, or nearing that goal. As advising psychiatrist, he says:

> No amount of mastery of factual information is sufficient for good human relationships. Leadership, in fact, essentially means outstanding ability in human relationships. Therefore, in a program of this kind, collaboration among educators, administrators, and clinically trained behavioral scientists seems to be not only appropriate but essential. Speaking for myself, I would say that it has worked and I have learned as much as I have contributed.

Below are some statements from fellows after they had finished their practicum:

> I found the leadership training program an unusual opportunity to reflect more deeply on the real role of the leader. On the job, we do not reflect enough. I feel much more strongly than I ever have before that teachers must become more scholarly. In order to stimulate kids to pursue knowledge, to ask questions, to think creatively, to understand themselves and others, we must become master scholars, equipped with scholarly skills.
>
> I have appreciated the fact that this has been an action course in which we have learned by doing. Through working with our interns and their respective principals, we have had the opportunity to test our skills in interpersonal relationships and to consider whether or not we are willing or able to cope with the problems of the supervisor or the principal.

Conclusion

Receptive top staff in nearby school systems enabled the development of an individual program for each fellow, a privilege that was much valued and appreciated by the University staff. Having a psychiatrist in the wings made it possible to risk using emotionally charged material: the fellows felt that writing and sharing their biographies was particularly valuable. The belief of the University in each fellow's capacity for growth and learning--once he has been freed to learn--has been reinforced each year. Freeing the learner is, of course, not a simple achievement, nor did the program succeed with all the fellows. To the extent that it did succeed, so did they.

ROLE AND FUNCTION OF SUPERVISORS AND CURRICULUM WORKERS

Rowannetta S. Allen

Former Assistant Superintendent of
Schools for Elementary Education
Prince Georges County, Maryland

The current period of sweeping changes in education is bringing about corresponding changes in the role of the supervisor and curriculum worker. This role, which at one time seemed clear-cut, is becoming more complex and could become more significant. The role is more complex because of the many persons at local, state and national levels who are actively demonstrating an interest in public education; it is potentially more significant because of the state of flux which currently characterizes curriculum development.

No longer is curriculum development a simple matter; this, too, is becoming more involved and often places the supervisor between the school system and the general public or serving as the agent of the school system to encourage public involvement and support. Inherent in the current situation is an urgent need for competent, courageous, professional leadership.

In the face of this challenge to educators to contribute vital leadership, there is an obvious lack of professional unity. In fact, there is apparent confusion among su-

---

Reprinted by permission from Educational Leadership, Vol. 23 (January, 1966), pp. 330-333.

pervisors and curriculum workers, as well as administrators, as to (a) the accepted purpose of supervision; (b) who is qualified to perform this function; and (c) how supervision shall be accomplished.

Need for Clarification

School systems differ, it is true, but with all of their differences, there is usually a singleness of purpose, namely, to provide the best possible education for children, youth, and adults served by the system. There is no single set of curriculum guides that can be used to prescribe a dynamic, changing program, nor can there be, if education is to keep abreast of the times. The urgent need of school systems throughout the country, therefore, is for an adequate number of professionally trained supervisors and curriculum workers who are prepared to assume leadership in continuing curriculum revision.

Supervisors and curriculum workers have been added to the administrative staffs of school systems purportedly to facilitate the development of and the implementation of improved educational programs. For example, as early as 1922-23, the State of Maryland, by act of the legislature, authorized the local units to employ "supervising teachers or helping teachers"[1] as professional appointees to the staff of the county superintendent of schools to assist him with the prescribed responsibilities of his office as expressed in the law: "The county superintendent shall visit the schools, observe the management and instruction and give suggestions for the improvement of the same."[2]

As public school systems recently have been confronted with the problems of providing for rapid increases in enroll-

1. _The Public School Laws of Maryland_, Vol. XXXIV (January, 1955), p. 137.

2. _Ibid._, p. 135.

ment and adjusting to the mobility which has accompanied this growth, many new job titles have appeared on the staff roster. Frequently existing personnel have been asked to assume new or additional responsibilities. In assuming the various titles assigned to them, and consequently performing the functions associated with the titles, the role of the supervisor and curriculum worker has often become ambiguous.

In material recently prepared by Gordon N. Mackenzie on "Roles of Supervisors and Curriculum Workers" there is confirmation of this:

> There is wide range in both the titles used and in the assignment of responsibilities to supervisors and curriculum workers. The diverse origins in the positions, some being in administration and others being in teaching, curriculum, and the improvement of instruction, cause initial difficulty. A strong supervisory or administrative lineage is apt to result as a stress on such functions as quality control, the provision of needed information for administrators, and the management and coordination of various kinds of organizational activities. The teaching, curricular, and instructional improvement lineage suggest a possible emphasis on direct assistance to teachers, curricular planning, and in-service education. The local variations in skills and interests of holders of various positions, and the differing patterns of organization further cloud the picture as to what any specific individuals do and how the supervisory and curriculum improvement functions are performed. In fact, to diagnose the manner in which supervisory and curriculum improvement functions are performed, it may be necessary in specific school systems to analyze the functioning of such diverse but related performers as the chief school administrator for instruction, directors, coordinators, general and specific subject supervisors, principals, building curriculum coordinators, and department heads.[3]

---

3. Gordon N. Mackenzie, "Roles of Supervisors and Curriculum Workers." Statement presented by Mackenzie as a former member of the ASCD Committee on Professionalization of Supervisors and Curriculum Workers for discussion by State ASCD groups.

Compounding the problem of identifying and clarifying the role of supervisors and curriculum workers, according to Mackenzie, are "the underdeveloped state of the theory of the fields of supervision and of curriculum as well as the low levels of preparation of some supervisors and curriculum workers. Certainly if there were well developed descriptive theories as to the nature of curriculum and of supervision, as areas of knowledge, there would be more clarity and understanding as to the functions which the workers in these areas could perform to maximize the output of the educational program. However, the present absence of this knowledge does not excuse the tendency on the part of many to oversimplify the nature of supervisory and curricular work and to assume that any good teacher, or any good administrator with sound professional intentions can perform the implied functions effectively."[4]

A little over a decade ago the purpose of supervision, as represented by a review of the titles listed in Education Index (June 1950-May 1955) and stated in general terms, were counseling teachers, helping beginning teachers, inspiring professional growth, improving instruction, and providing educational leadership. Ten years later the titles listed seem to indicate more purposes, more persons involved, more ways of getting supervision done and more inherent problems.

Emerging from the writings on supervision of this period are the questions: Whose responsibility is the improvement of instruction and the development of curriculum? Does this responsibility rest with the superintendent? the principal? the department head? the generalist? or the specialist?

Analysis and Description

In the recent literature there is a recognizable trend

---

4. Ibid., p. 2.

toward making curriculum development a cooperative undertaking and toward using a team approach to supervision. Each of these trends reinforces the urgent need for trained professional leadership to give direction and guidance to the group effort.

Some of the problems reflected in the titles appearing between 1950 and 1955 sound strangely familiar today. Mentioned among them were such problems as resolving conflicts in supervision, changing the attitude of teachers toward supervision, discovering an effective approach to supervision, agreement on basic principles of supervision, training for supervision, delineation of responsibilities, certification requirements, and group-centered supervision.

Newly stated, the concerns of a decade ago are still with us. Among them are the following: determining what techniques are worth while, effecting a wholesome balance in supervision, meeting the needs of experienced teachers as well as those of beginning teachers, up-dating the theory of supervision, human relations in supervision, clarifying the purpose of supervision and the roles of persons involved, how supervision is perceived, the "quest" of supervision, and the need for cooperation in supervision.

From a cursory review of the titles of articles on supervision, it is evident that there is growing interest in the topic, that supervision is being presented from many differing points of view, that the volume of writing on supervision is increasing, and that most of the current writers are new to the field.

Obviously the literature deals more with an analysis and description of supervision as it exists rather than of supervision as it ought to be. Constantly recurring is an expression of the need for clarification of role.

This is further substantiated by Roy Wahle's review of titles of dissertations listed in _Research Studies in Education_ for the period 1957 through 1962. While serving as a member of the ASCD Committee on Professionalization of Supervisors and Curriculum Workers, Wahle prepared a report which reveals a total of eighty-four dissertation titles dealing with varied aspects of supervision and curriculum development. Of this total nearly a third deal with role, status, and duties of the different persons performing the supervisory function. These include the principal, the general supervisor, the instructional vice-principal, the superintendent, and, in the case of student teachers, the supervising teacher. Nineteen titles relate to techniques, activities, services, and practices of instructional supervisors. A third major group of titles centers around studies of supervisory relationships, perceptions, and attitudes.

Implicit in these titles is the continuing need for clarifying the role of the supervisor and curriculum worker. The local variations in assignment of supervisory functions mentioned by Mackenzie are evident here, and while not mentioned specifically as problems, there is the recurrence of such key words and phrases as attitudinal perceptions, administrative organization, leadership, cooperative programs, critical competencies, principles and basic assumptions, personal characteristics, competency patterns, and in-service education.

Out of this situation what can arise?

In a previous article in Educational Leadership, Harold Shafer called the attention of supervisors and curriculum workers to the Flexner report, suggesting that the experience of the medical profession in achieving professionalization may offer a perspective to engage educators in active pursuit of comparable standards as a professional group.

Professionalization implies the possession of a certain and particular know-how which can be brought to bear on problems. It implies concerted action to raise the level of practice within the profession and to maintain a mutually acceptable level of performance through policies enforced by the professional group. It implies selective admissions, specialized training in duly accredited institutions, and certification procedures approximating licensing.

As we realize the urgency of the need for trained professional leadership in education and as we become more keenly aware of the unanswered problems which could be resolved if we, as a profession, took action, is it too much to hope that we may strengthen our efforts in that direction now?

Succeeding articles by members of the ASCD Committee on Professionalization of Supervisors and Curriculum Workers will alert readers to existing conditions and will suggest some reasonable possibilities for concerted action.

THE PRINCIPAL AS A COUNTERPUNCHER

Ray Cross

Associate Professor of Educational Administration

University of Minnesota
Minneapolis, Minnesota

As a raw youth, I decided that my appropriate field of athletic endeavor was boxing. A few bouts, however, persuaded me that this ambition had been ill conceived and that my true forte lay in games requiring less bodily contact, say, table tennis or shuffleboard. Nevertheless, during my brief tenure as an ineffective gladiator, I acquired a concept that I have since concluded has application to the elementary school principal's world--the concept of counterpunching.

Counterpunching, as a pugilistic strategy, consists of taking advantage of the openings afforded by the opponent's attacks. The counterpuncher lets the opponent take initiative, parries his thrusts, and clobbers him while he is exposed. Although many boxers have enjoyed considerable success with this kind of strategy, I am convinced that elementary school principals who consistently use this approach will eventually find themselves flat on the canvas, metaphorically speaking.

Although it is to be hoped that principals do not engage in counterpunching in the literal sense, they often

---

Reprinted by permission from _National Elementary Principal_, Vol. 51 (October, 1971), pp. 26-29.

function in an environment in which they are constantly countering the initiatives of others. Counterpunching for the elementary school principal consists of responding to requests, appeals, demands, and complaints of the many people who look to him as the school's ultimate decision maker. Counterpunching suggests reaction rather than action, and struggle for survival rather than growth.

I realize that a certain amount of counterpunching is inherent in the principal's role. He cannot retreat to an ivory tower, refusing to deal with the less glamorous problems of everyday school life. I am concerned, however, that too many principals have the opposite problem; they become so enmeshed in the day-to-day problems that they are unable to perform the critical tasks of leadership. A principal severely afflicted by the counterpunching syndrome is dealing almost entirely with issues raised by others, each of whom is concerned with only a part of the school operation or with his own personal interests. When a principal responds only to issues raised by others, his actions become random movements in terms of the direction of the school program as a whole.

All principals, I think, are aware that they are counterpunching some of the time. The results of two recent studies on the problems of elementary school principals suggest that many principals may be counterpunching most of the time.[1,2] Both studies viewed elementary school principals within a problem/decision framework. Observers shadowed elementary school principals, recording and classifying the problems that came up for a decision. These studies had several focuses, but each documented the origins of princi-

---

1. Ray Cross and Vernon Bennett. "Problem Situations Encountered by School Principals in Different Socio-Economic Settings." A paper presented at the American Educational Research Association, February 8, 1969, Los Angeles, California.

2. Ray Cross. "A Description of Decision-Making Patterns of Elementary School Principals." (In process.)

pal's' problems according to the three categories for executive decision discussed by Chester I. Barnard in his classic book on administration.[3] Barnard suggests that administrative problems can be classified in terms of three distinct origins.

One occasion for administrative decision is upon receipt of instructions from, or general requirements of, superior authority. For example: A principal receives notice from the state education authority that at least three fire drills must be held annually. A number of decisions by the principal must stem from this one order, such as when to hold drills and which children should leave which exit. Administrative problems of this type are classified as intermediary problems.

A case is referred to the administrator by subordinates in the organization. Such occasions may arise from the inability or unwillingness of the subordinates to make a decision, from novel conditions, conflict of justification, or lack of clarity in policy. Examples of this kind of decision are all too plentiful:

The first-grade teacher reports that Ralph has brought his dog to school again and asks the principal what to do about it.

or

The school counselor and social worker sharply disagree about their respective roles and request that the principal arbitrate the matter.

Such issues, referred to principals by teachers, pupils, and parents, are classified as appellate problems.

The third and final occasion for decision originates with the administrator. His own understanding of a situation leads him to decide whether something ought to be done or corrected. According to Barnard, such occasions are the most significant indicators of an administrator's most im-

---

3. Chester I. Barnard. The Function of the Executive. Cambridge, Massachusetts: Harvard University Press, 1938.

portant obligation to raise those issues that no one else can or will. Examples:

The principal notes that reading achievement scores in the primary unit have slipped and calls the primary teachers together to discuss causes and possible remedies.

or

The principal believes that the involvement of a team of teachers in hiring new staff will result in greater collegial support of new teachers, and he initiates a structure for such involvement.

When such activities are initiated by the principal, they are classified as creative problems.

In one of two studies mentioned earlier,[4] Cross and Bennett explored the nature of elementary school principals' problems and their variability with the school's socioeconomic setting:

Origins of Principals' Problems in High and Low Socioeconomic Settings

Problem Origin	High Socioeconomic Setting % of Problems	Low Socioeconomic Setting % of Problems
Appellate	41	61
Intermediary	6	7
Creative	53	32

These data indicate that, taken as a whole, principals of schools in low socioeconomic communities are particularly burdened with appellate problems. As one might expect, it appears that appellate problems "drive out" creative problems, since principals in "high" settings had 53 percent creative problems and principals in "low" settings had only 32 percent creative problems. Neither group was often confronted with intermediary problems--6 percent for principals

4. See footnote 1.

in "high" settings and 7 percent for principals in "low" settings. Thus, if we accept intermediary and appellate problems as instances of counterpunching, principals of schools in low socioeconomic settings were counterpunching on 68 percent of their problems, and principals of schools in high socioeconomic settings on only 47 percent of theirs.

An interesting sidelight of this study is the large volume of problems that confronted the principals each day. Principals in both high and low socioeconomic settings worked with an average of approximately 100 problems a day. Thus, the percentages mentioned above are fairly accurate indicators of problem frequencies in raw numbers.

A study still in progress has reinforced the above findings.[5] In this study, it was found that a group of principals in inner-city elementary schools had a problem origin distribution of 68 percent appellate, 12 percent intermediary, and 20 percent creative. This very closely parallels the percentage distribution for principals in "low" settings in the first study mentioned.

It should not be assumed that the socioeconomic level of the school's community completely controls the origins of the principal's problems. Within each of the groups of principals in the Cross and Barnard study, there were variations in problem origin distributions. In some of the schools in high socioeconomic settings, the principals dealt with a high percentage of counterpunching problems.

As I have said, I think that it is neither possible nor desirable for principals to avoid appellate and intermediary problems completely. I do think, however, that if principals intend to exercise educational leadership, they should reduce appellate and intermediary problems to 40 percent of the total number.

For principals of schools in the inner city, additional administrative assistance is probably necessary to relieve them from the press of appellate problems. Many large school

---

5. See footnote 2.

systems have moved in this direction during the past few years. The Minneapolis public schools, for example, now staff their inner-city elementary schools with assistant principals and administrative interns.

Additional administrative staff is not, however, the only possible solution for the principal who would like to trade some of his appellate problems for leadership opportunities. The power to do this is at the disposal of every principal. To some extent, each principal must prescribe his own antidote for the counterpunching syndrome. I would, however, like to offer the following suggestions to principals who are interested in reducing an overload of appellate and intermediary problems:

1. Assess your own pattern of problems. A useful starting point is to acquire some assessment of the problems with which you are now dealing. Who originates them? What is their nature? Are they the types of problems you would like to work with? A log kept over a week's period should provide a reliable assessment.

2. Avoid solving problems that can best be handled by others. Daniel E. Griffiths has set forth the proposition that an administrator's effectiveness is inversely proportional to the number of decisions he personally makes concerning the affairs of the organization.[6] Even though teachers in general are seeking wider responsibilities, many individual faculty members have been conditioned to seek the principal's judgement on every matter of significance. Although playing the role of Mr. Wonderful Decision Maker may do a great deal for a principal's ego, usually such a role leads to overly dependent teachers and overwhelmed principals. I am *not* suggesting that principals turn a deaf ear to teachers who

---

6. Daniel E. Griffiths. *Administrative Theory*. New York: Appleton-Century-Crofts, 1959, p. 89.

are seeking help. I am suggesting that principals may sometimes need to provide a different form of help from that of making a teacher's decision for him. If Miss Newcomer is sending all of her discipline problems to the principal for his decision, perhaps the best course of action for the principal is to see that Miss Newcomer acquires the skills needed to make her own discipline decisions.

3. Set up structures that will provide bases for decisions to be made without your attention. I once observed a principal who, during a period of minutes, was asked by four teachers whether it was too cold to take children outside for physical education. Apparently, it had not occurred to him to establish guidelines that would permit teachers themselves to make this kind of decision.
4. Delegate. Many of the tasks for which a principal is directly responsible do not really require a high level of professional competence. The willingness of a principal to assign tasks, such as routine reports to secretaries, clerks, and aides, can lighten the minutia load considerably. Although he may be ultimately responsible for such reports, it does not follow that the principal must perform the simple clerical tasks necessary to complete them.
5. Seek opportunities to turn appellate and intermediary problems into creative ones. Such a strategy is available to a principal who looks beyond the immediate problem to its larger possibilities and implications. For instance, in the previously cited example of a principal who was called on to arbitrate the role conflict between a counselor and social worker, the principal might choose to form a pupil personnel team that would include the two parties to the conflict. Such a move could not only remove the conflict but could also enhance pupil personnel services through a more coordinated effort.

Relieving the overburden of appellate and intermediary problems is not, of course, an end in itself. It offers the principal only a means of freeing himself for leadership tasks. There is no doubt, however, that for many principals amelioration of the counterpunching malady is a prerequisite that has remained too long ignored.

COOPERATIVE ADMINISTRATION

James Greig

Administrative Career Program
Harvard Graduate School of Education
Harvard University

and

Robert R. Lee

Administrative Career Program
Harvard Graduate School of Education
Harvard University

The increased focus on elementary education by professional and lay persons throughout the country is one of the most encouraging results of the present ferment in education. This more solid recognition of the value of the elementary school has important implications for the elementary school principal as well.

In the past, writers have customarily spoken of the principal as the key person in the school system, and some have referred to him as an educational statesman. Unfortunately, such eulogies have been largely aspirations for the principal rather than descriptions of him. Now, however, serious issues emanating from forces at home and abroad are confronting the elementary school and the elementary school principal with the insistent demand for practical solutions to complex problems. Hence, the myth of the past has become the reality of the present. The school principal is

---

Reprinted by permission from National Elementary Principal, Vol. 44 (January, 1965), pp. 71-65.

the key person in the educational enterprise and may yet become, in every sense of the word, an educational statesman.

At a time when social change is rapidly transforming many of our institutions in order to meet the demands of a greater society, the principal has the clear responsibility of examining his own role in the context of change. For many years, he has been the instrument for effecting educational change, but the time seems appropriate for a transformation of the principalship itself. Undoubtedly, the role of the principal has progressed from "first teacher" to "school manager" to "instructional leader." The last stage of this evolution hopefully reflects the principal's most significant contribution to education, although the importance of administration should not be demeaned. However, a central question must still be raised: Has the essential pattern of the principalship been modified to fit the principal for dealing with the emergent forces which now confront him? Change is not always desirable, even though novelty often has a perverse attraction. Yet without an awareness of the need to adapt to major social reconstructions, the individual is less able to function adequately in the new environment. Such are the dynamic dimensions of the current educational scene that it is highly probable that the elementary school principalship will soon enter upon yet another stage in its development. The usual vertical relationship of the principal in the school organization is likely to broaden into a more formal horizontal relationship which will greatly influence his role and give new significance.

The major premise of this discussion is that cooperative teaching has some viable lessons for administration and supervision. A rather natural extension of this emerging pattern of staff organization is cooperative administration, in which term we include supervision as well. The concept of administration has already gone through several stages of development, and perhaps school administration will be expanded to include more formal collaboration among administrators than heretofore. It might well be argued that the effectiveness of a single principal with his individual perceptions, competencies, and leadership style could be increased through cooperative activities in planning, guiding, and evaluating as a team member.

To provide a rationale for this different perspective on school administration, it is necessary to determine which characteristics of cooperative teaching can be applied analogously to cooperative administration. Theoretically, the educational increments which are reported as a result of team teaching are also potential in team supervision. At the present, this form of administrative organization is not sufficiently widespread to provide empirical evidence for its usefulness in improving the quality of education in general. However, the theoretical rationale for cooperative teaching gives us some justification for speculating about the possibilities inherent in principal teams.

Shaplin defines team teaching as "a type of instructional organization, involving teaching personnel and the students assigned to them, in which two or more teachers are given responsibility, working together, for all or a significant part of the . . . instruction of the same group of students."[1]

What, then, is cooperative administration? For the purpose of this presentation, the definition might be altered to read: Cooperative administration and supervision is a type of organization involving administrative personnel and the staff assigned to them in which two or more principals have the responsibility for working together with the same group of teachers for all or a significant part of the time.

Although the definition which emerges from this paraphrasing is not too precise, at least a new perspective is achieved. By this definition, the team consists of two or three principals who have a more or less formal relationship guaranteed by the organization of the school system. Thus,

---

1. Judson T. Shaplin and Henry F. Olds, Jr., eds. Team Teaching. New York: Harper & Row, Publishers, 1964, p. 15.

the typical model of a school principal working only with his own staff is being set aside for purposes of discussion.

Critics of conventional school organization speak somewhat disparagingly of the "self-contained" classroom and the "egg crate" school. Whether or not such pejorative terms are justifiable, they force us to examine organization more critically. For that matter, the concept of a self-contained _school_ may be equally open to thoughtful criticism. The common assumption about a school is that it is a more or less self-sufficient unit consisting of a principal, teachers, pupils, and parents with a number of avenues to the outside world via curriculum councils, interschool visitations, principals' meetings, and so on. In this concept, there are both geographical and psychological barriers in our thinking about schools which cast them in comparative isolation.

It seems reasonable to posit that the concept of the isolated school unit is already being eroded by numerous forces acting singly or together. The present focus on school integration has led to such schemes as the pairing of schools, as in the Princeton Plan, and the busing of children--both of which shift student population around and affect individual schools. Also, educational parks are being developed which, though composed of discrete buildings, provide a togetherness. These and other plans are impinging on the isolated school.

This has obvious bearing on the function of the principals in the schools involved. In the Princeton Plan, although no one has mentioned it, team supervision with each administrator bringing his specific skills to bear on various problems is potential and might thereby improve the quality of school administration. Pooling teachers, as opposed to assigning them to separate school faculties, would maximize the possibility of better staff utilization and satisfy the needs of teachers to a greater degree, to say nothing of the benefit to the pupils. This pooling of teachers may also mollify the critics who maintain that certain schools are automatically given new or poor teachers, thereby resulting in inferior education for those children in their care. In educational parks, the team approach in administration could lead to better and smoother articulation between elementary and middle schools, and possibly between middle and high schools, which in most cases is presently inadequate.

It seems reasonable to argue, therefore, that the isolated school, even in a large school system, might in some ways be as inadequate as the self-contained classroom. Similarly, the solitary principal might function at reduced effectiveness because of the constraint imposed upon him by the traditional school organization.

At least two objections will be raised at this point. First, the situation is being overstated since provision is made in most school systems for regular inter-school communication. Second, the solitary individual is a myth and even if he were not, excessive togetherness reduces individuality and initiative which are the essential ingredients of a vigorous educational enterprise. With due consideration given these objections, there still appears considerable doubt that our contemporary school organization with respect to the school principal is a product of deliberate thought. At the present, habit rather than carefully considered planning appears to be dominant. By implication, cooperative administration might serve to redefine the school principalship and provide a vehicle for removing the psychological barriers separating schools.

Some other underlying assumptions concerning cooperative administration should be made explicit.

First, we believe that certain educational objectives can be more readily achieved by a team effort. Thus, cooperative administration must not be thought of in isolation from specific goals achievable by collaboration. No purpose is served by an administrative organization whose structure is totally divorced from its objectives. It is as true in educational administration as it is in architecture that form and function are inseparable.

Second, the number of schools within the system imposes

definite limitations as well as potentialities for cooperative administration. We believe, however, that even a small system of only two schools might benefit from continuous collaborative activities.

Third, the precise role of the principal in this new arrangement cannot be defined. The team structure and the personality of each member of the team will in large measure define the actual role of each participant.

It is essential now to turn our attention specifically to three basic questions?

1. How might cooperative administration improve the principalship?
2. What models of team structure are available?
3. What are the prospects for the adoption of such a scheme?

The case for or against cooperative administration depends upon valid answers to these questions. The suggested answers in this paper may serve to stir up discussion, even if they do not provide definite answers.

Question: How Might Cooperative Administration Improve the Principalship?

A _formal_ arrangement to promote cooperative activities by teams of principals is not yet a widespread pattern in most school systems, even where team teaching is practiced. Yet, as has already been intimated, a structure involving two or more principals working together as a team suggests some possible advantages as well as disadvantages.

If cooperative effort by teachers improves the effectiveness of planning, supervision and evaluation activities of principals might also be improved by collaboration. The opportunity within the team structure to define objectives clearly would do much to reduce generalized professional opinions to substantive definitions. Where each individual is forced to make explicit his assumptions and values, the process of rational deliberation is greatly facilitated. Thus, the planning phase of the principal's responsibilities might well be accomplished with greater skill as a result of including the perceptions of other principals. A team does not automatically guarantee more perceptive planning, but the group process can be a useful lens through which objectives, plans, and procedures can be viewed with deeper insight and clarity. Brief, informal contacts among principals do not appear to be an adequate substitute for cooperative planning on a continuing basis.

The dimensions of cooperative planning might include the combined staff, pupils, and facilities of two or three schools. This may not be as horrendous as it first sounds. The pool of talent which a combined staff affords is often obscured by the traditional "self-contained" school concept. The cooperative planning of people, time, space, and facilities from this widened perspective provides numerous alternatives for a group of imaginative principals. If we include ancillary personnel under the direction of the principals, such as supervisors and subprofessional individuals, then the planning operation is all the more powerful and leads to instructional leadership of a high order. Although the broadened concept of cooperative administration of a cluster of two or more schools is not invulnerable to criticism, there is some organization from its stultifying rigidity.

The improvement of classroom instruction is a significant part of the principal's total responsibility. Undoubtedly, the supervisory activities are often both the most satisfying and frustrating of the numerous functions that the principal performs. One of the most potent forces at work at the present time which handicaps the principal from providing effective leadership is the dynamic change in knowledge and curriculum. New methods and materials are constantly emerging, and professional judgement must be given on many important issues without the prerequisite background to make a firm judgement. Moreover, the elementary principal is often a generalist who develops special interest in one or two subjects where direct experience or study has given him an increased measure of competence. In many phases of the school program, his contribution is, of necessity, negligible and no amount of "pedaguese" can totally obscure this fact. The principal is bombarded on all sides by new programs in reading, mathematics, science, and so on, as well as new methodology, including technological aids. Indeed, the principal is fortunate if he possesses expertise in one or two specific areas.

Thus, the dynamic condition of knowledge with concomitant changes in method and media mandate that the principal have the opportunity to provide more leadership in the areas of his special training and interest. Cooperative administration might provide such an opportunity. The modern "math" principal, the "ITA" principal, and the "kitchen physics" principal might combine to present a more complete instructional force. If principals are going to keep professionally up-to-date and remain in the vanguard of progress, ways of maximizing their time must be found.

Finally, the principal is called upon to evaluate the work of the teachers in his school and often with them the school program. Evaluation of teacher effectiveness is one of the most crucial and yet most difficult tasks confronting the elementary school principal. Even though evaluation implies more than mere "inspection" or measurement against some arbitrary standard, this form of educational leadership produces the most conflicts and tension in the principal-teacher relationship. In large measure, the teacher views evaluation as a hindrance to professional autonomy.

Is evaluation, in principle, compatible with the dignity of the fully developed profession which teaching aspires to become? Undoubtedly. Some form of evaluation is essential and desirable. The obligation on the part of the principal, therefore, is to assure the teacher that his evaluation is conducive to the teacher's professional growth. Mere slogans about democratic supervision are clearly inadequate when the principal-evaluator makes no sincere attempt to effect productive and satisfying changes in the performances of the teacher himself. This is one of the foremost challenges in educational administration.

It is believed that the diversified perceptions of several teachers produce a more viable evaluation of pupil performance. Analogously, the viewpoints of several administrators might give a more accurate picture of a teacher's performance. Teachers might respond to this multiple evaluation with greater enthusiasm as the possibilities of principal bias are diminished. The danger of oversupervision should not be overlooked. However, the use of multiple evaluators might be a safeguard against the erosion of teacher professionalism and morale.

Question: What Models of Team Structure Are Available?

A natural sequel to the consideration of the improvement of the principalship by cooperative administration would be speculation as to the types of functional administrative team models.

Luvern Cunningham in an article published in 1960 suggested that teaching teams could be divided into four general categories.[2] Using equivalent terminology one can readily adapt three of these categories to administrative teams in the following manner:

1. Team-leader type. This generally refers to a team with a hierarchical authority structure involving a designated leader and other possible roles in the vertical authority structure. A typical model of this type might be a principal with expertise in a given area (curriculum) to assume the role of administrative team leader, with two other principals as

2. Luvern L. Cunningham. "Team Teaching: Where Do We Stand?" Chicago: Midwest Administration Center, The University of Chicago. Administrators Notebook, April 1960.

senior administrator(s). The aforementioned would constitute the line, whereas supervisors (where they exist in school systems) acting in an advisory capacity would constitute the staff.

This model conceives of the supervisors as being under the jurisdiction of the principals as well as the central office. This last arrangement would provide maximum assistance, feedback, and articulation among and to schools in addition to the central office. It would also be necessary to assign the supervisory staff to a given number of linked schools rather than have them supervise all schools at given levels. However, in this model, it is mandatory that there be this vertical authority structure with one designated leader for stipulated task areas, who acts as the final decision maker.

Conceivably, this organization provides for continuing direction in the achievement of the educational objectives of the group. However, this organization might also result in the greatest amount of dysfunctional tensions and conflict.

2. Associate-type team. In this type of cooperative supervision, the major difference is that all team members have equal status with no designated leader. This implies a pooling of talent and a group of final decision makers in contrast to a single decision maker in the team leader administrative model. This does not mean that all principals must have the same amount of experience and expertise in administration. In fact, diversity might vitalize the team efforts.

   The advantage of this model over the team-leader type model is that principals might feel less threatened by the loss of status. Another advantage is the inherent flexibility in the organization, which permits the emergence of special competencies as specific tasks arise.

3. Experienced administrator - beginning administrator type team. All too often, newly appointed, inexperienced principals have not had the opportunity of working with more than one man while learning the job. This type of team suggests that the new principal work with all the members of a team for a given period of time in order to gain insights into different leadership styles. His work with the team as a whole might provide a superior kind of induction for a beginning principal.

Some schools have administrative trainees who do not operate in an administrative team but rather with one principal. The anticipated outcome of team involvement is that better administrators will be produced, with more understanding of the many ways different problems might be handled and of the alternatives that are available. The rationale is that much valuable time is wasted by administrators casting alternatives or not being able to perceive a number of good alternatives in the decision making process. We feel that, through this experience, the intern-administrator would be able to make quicker and better decisions, but it would certainly offer a better framework for decision making.

These models are merely suggestive of the types of teams now used in team teaching which have had varying degrees of success in actual operation. Additional research into the functioning of these teams would certainly improve the formulation of a theoretical framework for cooperative administration. The Palo Alto unified school district[3] has done some tentative work in this area which promises to offer empirical evidence in support of these or other models.

---

3. Nicholas J. Anastasiow and Abraham S. Fischler. "A Proposal for Teaming Principals." National Elementary Principal, Vol. 44 (November, 1964), pp. 59-64.

The selection of a model of organization would depend on the goals that need to be achieved. Certain factors, we feel, would strongly influence the type of model viz.:

1. geographical location;
2. special competencies of administrators; and
3. experience of the administrators.

The proximity of schools would be the obvious factor for convenience, as in the case of pairing for racial balance, and for maximum contact. However, this could be overridden by the special competencies of administrators when needed for specific tasks--for example, the introduction of a new mathematics program into the curriculum by a principal versed in this field. Experience emerges as a factor in the training of embryo administrators or the induction of new administrators.

Question: What Are the Prospects for the Adoption of Such a Scheme?

It should be obvious that there are inherent difficulties in the use of such models of administrative organization. There are a number of questions which suggest themselves with respect to cooperative administration.

1. Will the traditional resistance to change maintain the status quo?
2. What will the potential conflicts be that would render this type of organization dysfunctional?
3. What will be the effect of cooperative administration on the staff and students?
4. How will school-community relationships be affected by the team structure?
5. What difficulties in administrative arrangements will manifest themselves in such areas as scheduling, teacher assignments, grouping, etc.?
6. Is the efficiency of such an arrangement questionable?
7. How will this affect relationships with the superintendent?

It is hoped that these questions will stimulate experimental programs, other than those now in existence, in various school systems across the country. Hopefully, reasonable solutions will be forthcoming which will lead to better theoretical frameworks of cooperative administration. Critical issues in education today mandate that school systems share their perceptions of new patterns of school organizations.

The vicissitudes of the times are modifying many of the traditional institutions of our society; education, itself, is in transition. More particularly, administrative theory is changing, and new concepts are emerging. New staff patterns, greater use of schools as vehicles of social mobility combine to introduce new dimensions in both the task and organization of the elementary school today. Hopefully, the principal, as the key person in the elementary school, will fulfill his role more adequately than heretofore.

THE ADMINISTRATIVE TEAM IN SUPERVISION

Maurice E. St. Mary

Principal, Forest Road School
Valley Stream, New York

The major goal of any school administrative staff is the improvement of instruction. Unfortunately, with the growth in school population, a great number of administrators have become so bogged down with other responsibilities that they have not had time to think about this instructional goal or, if they have thought of it, they have not had time to do much about it.

In our school district, however, the administrative staff have managed to keep instruction as their primary aim --even in the midst of rapid expansion and the resulting administrative problems. This was accomplished by using a team approach to supervision.

This approach involves organizing the administrative-supervisory staff so that all principals and supervisors spend some time in each building in the district. Normally, a principal is responsible, along with whatever supervisors are on the staff, for supervising the instruction in his particular building. He has sole responsibility for evaluating teachers, advising on curriculum revisions and, in some instances, for hiring or releasing personnel. In our district, however, the team approach is used for all these functions.

We have been using this team approach for thirteen years

Reprinted by permission from *National Elementary Principal*, Vol. 45 (April, 1966), pp. 59-61.

and feel that it has a great number of advantages over the traditional building principal concept. We offer a full explanation of our plan so that other administrators may judge for themselves.

The district described here is Union Free School District No. 30, one of three elementary districts in Valley Stream, Long Island, New York. There are three main schools in the district and a three-room neighborhood school serving a total of 2,300 pupils from kindergarten to grade six. The population of the district is 17,000. The teaching staff numbers 114, and the administrative team includes a supervising principal, three building principals, an assistant principal, and an elementary consultant.

Responsibilities of the Team

Under our plan, building principals not only are responsible for a particular building but also have district-wide responsibilities. As part of the team, they supervise instruction in their own buildings and also share supervision of instruction throughout the district.

Teacher observation and evaluation. Until 1958, every teacher was seen by each member of the team in a formal observation. Thus, each teacher received five formal observations from five administrators with five different backgrounds. Since 1959, each principal observes every teacher in his building at least once, preferably more. The elementary consultant and the assistant principal observe each tenure teacher in the district at least once and each probationary teacher at least twice. Each principal, the assistant principal, and the elementary consultant observe all probationary teachers in the district as follows: (1) each teacher in his first year, by December 1; (2) each teacher in his second year, by February 1; and (3) each teacher in his third year, by January 1. In addition, each principal observes tenure teachers outside his own building upon the recommendation of any of the other observers.

This system has been extremely effective. Several resources can be brought to bear on any particular teacher's problem, and the good things teachers are doing can more easily be shared with other teachers in the district. An administrator feels more confident when tenure time is near for a teacher because he knows that it is not only his judgement which decides for or against tenure. The team decisions are made carefully, and teachers are thus protected to some extent against unfair judgement.

Selecting and orienting teachers. All administrators are jointly responsible for interviewing and selecting new personnel. When a teacher is offered a position, he is informed of the district's team approach to supervision so he will know what is expected of him and what he can expect of the administrators. He is also told that he is hired for the district and not for any particular school. Thus we are able each year to balance the staffs so that no one school is overloaded with inexperienced personnel and so that each has a proportionate number of experienced teachers.

Once new personnel have been secured, the team orients them to the district by several specially planned meetings. These sessions cover district philosophy, lesson planning, classroom control, and the use of multiple texts in social studies and science.

After they are in the classroom, new teachers are observed early and frequently--as noted above--and they are given aid when, and if, they need it. Asking for help is considered a mark of maturity, and teachers are assured that the administrators believe that it is their job to serve the staff.

Curriculum committees. Curriculum committees are handled in a similar manner. Each administrator is assigned as a consultant to a committee which is working on a curriculum area in which he has appropriate background. The administrator helps the committee with problems and provides resource materials. He also serves as the liaison between the committee and the administrative team, keeping the other administrators informed of the committee's activities and helping to have the committee's work put in written form for the rest of the staff. Among the accomplishments of these curriculum committees have been courses of study in social studies and science and a parents' bulletin on homework.

There are about six grade-level meetings for all teachers each year. They have proved to be a fine avenue for sharing ideas and for getting the thinking of all teachers of the district on problems affecting a certain grade level. A member of the administrative team is assigned to each of these grade-level groups to perform the same functions as he does for the curriculum committees and also to provide liaison with teachers at other grade levels.

Coordination of summer work. Members of the administrative team work an eleven-month year. Teamwork again pays dividends during the summer months for it is at this time that the vast majority of new courses of study are typed, collated, and readied for the opening of school in September. The vacations of team members are scheduled so that at least one administrator is always on duty during the summer months. All members are present for the two weeks immediately after the close of school, and at this time the summer work is planned. In the same manner, all are on hand for the week preceding the opening of school in the fall so that an assessment can be made of the work done during the summer.

In the summer of 1957, some forty different handbooks, booklets, and instruction sheets were typed, duplicated, and collated. The work of the team in the summer months is described in more detail in another article.[1]

---

1. Maurice E. St. Mary, "Eleven Months for School Administrators," _American School Board Journal_, Vol. 136 (June, 1958), pp. 27-28.

Can Others Duplicate This Program?

The question in many readers' minds may be, "Will such a program work in my school district?" We believe it can--although, of course, modifications would have to be made in larger districts.[2] Perhaps a brief discussion of the reactions why we feel our administrative team plan has worked will suggest the hazards for which other districts should watch.

First, the administrative team is a highly cooperative group and works effectively as a team. Our district had the example of the supervising principal who was the only principal in the district before the great migration of city people to the suburbs. He had foresight enough to plan ahead for when the new schools were opened. He secured administrators who he knew would cooperate to make the team approach a success. Therefore, the team is a cooperative group of people who are not overly sensitive to criticism. Rather than being taken as a personal affront, criticism is viewed as an effort to improve the educational program. Ideas are discussed openly at the weekly principals' meetings. Arguments may take place, but no one goes away from the meetings with any animosity toward another member of the team. Ideas may come from anyone on the team or any other member of the staff. Actually, no one person can take full credit for any accomplishment because many people have a hand in translating ideas into policy.

Second, all members of the team are constantly and thoroughly well informed about the district's program. The weekly meetings of the administrative team help in this regard and are ideal for solving problems as they arise--and, in many cases, before they arise. In this way, all administrators

---

2. Editor's note: For further discussion of administrative teams, see: Nicholas J. Anastasiow and Abraham S. Fischler, "A Proposal for Teaming Principals," National Elementary Principal, Vol. 44 (November, 1964), pp. 59-64 and James Greig and Robert R. Lee, "Cooperative Administration," National Elementary Principal, Vol. 44 (January, 1965), pp. 71-76.

are kept informed about all phases of the district's educational program.

Third, all members of the team keep abreast of community and board of education attitudes. All administrators attend the monthly meetings of the board of education and thus are informed about how board members feel toward various issues and become acquainted with them. All of this helps to build a highly cooperative relationship.

In our district, the team approach has paid many dividends--to the individual members of the team, to all members of the staff, and, most important, to the boys and girls who attend our schools.

GUIDELINES FOR CURRICULUM DEVELOPMENT

Clayton E. Buell

Supervisor, Instructional Services
The School District of Philadelphia
Philadelphia, Pennsylvania

For more than twenty years there has been widespread consensus that the curriculum is best developed and installed by the cooperative group method. The 1951 yearbook of the Association for Supervision and Curriculum Development stated that although a curriculum developed by a committee working alone provided much help to committee members who produced it, "the material has little value to teachers who have not participated in its development."[1]

This cooperative group method of curriculum development consists of giving to all teachers opportunities to contribute to the solving curriculum, but centering the greater responsibility in the hands of a smaller group referred to as the curriculum committee. The method is effective because when teachers contribute to the development of the curriculum--or when they know they have a genuine opportunity to contribute to and affect it--they are much more likely to accept and use it.

Even though the cooperative group method for curriculum development has been largely accepted, a comprehensive list

---

Reprinted by permission from Educational Leadership, Vol. II (December, 1968), pp. 293-297.

1. Association for Supervision and Curriculum Development. Action for Curriculum Improvement. Washington, D.C.: the Association, 1951, p. 90.

of procedural guidelines has not been assembled by any one writer. Rather, different authors state specific procedures that they consider to be important.

Guidelines for Change

A search of the literature in curriculum development was made by the writer to discover guidelines and their use in developing curriculum guides. There seemed to be agreement on the fourteen listed here. Explanations of the guidelines are given and the relationship of each to curriculum development is considered.

Guideline 1. Teachers should first be aware of a need for change.

If the curriculum is to be improved, there must first be a desire for change, according to writers in the field. As Miel says, "dissatisfaction with existing conditions seems to be a prerequisite for intentional change."[2]

Caswell and Associates agree, as they state, "When city-wide curriculum planning comes as a natural response to expressed needs in the local school, it automatically becomes a part of the local school program, and it needs no artificial stimulation."[3]

If a program of curriculum improvement is to be successful, many teachers and staff members must be sensitized to the need for change. The leadership in the program may well capitalize on minor complaints of teachers and direct these immediate dissatisfactions into a positive direction so that teachers may see curriculum revision as a solution.

---

2. Alice Miel. Changing the Curriculum: A Social Process. New York: D. Appleton Century Company, Inc., 1946, p. 40.

3. Hollis L. Caswell and Associates. Curriculum Improvement in Public School Systems. New York: Bureau of Publications, Teachers College, Columbia University, 1950, p. 168.

Guideline 2. <u>The central office should provide leadership in coordinating the activities of various instructional workers so that a unified curriculum is developed</u>.

Central office leadership should be available as curriculum development begins, and should help to originate process. As Anderson states, "Some have made the mistake of believing that a democratic leader waits for the teachers to ask to initiate a program of curriculum study."[4]

According to Caswell and Associates, it is the job of the central office to "provide leadership in continuing analysis of curriculum programs and needs and in the formulation of a comprehensive program to meet them."[5]

Guideline 3. <u>Adequate resources should be provided</u>.

Resources provided by the central office should be of different types. As Abrams suggests, "The organization will make available to its members the necessary material facilities, time, human resources, and financial aid."[6]

Material facilities may include professional books, courses of study from other places, textbooks and reference books, meeting rooms, and secretarial supplies and equipment. Time may refer to the provision made for personnel to work during the school day. Human resources may be staff members, teachers, consultants, leaders, and secretaries. Financial aid may include provision made for substitute teachers who free regular teachers during the day so that meetings may be held on school time, for payment for time spent after school hours or Saturday meetings, for payment during summer months for writing, for consultation services and for materials and books needed.

Guideline 4. <u>The guide should be prepared by a group</u>

---

4. Vernon E. Anderson. <u>Principles and Procedures of Curriculum Improvement</u>. New York: The Ronald Press Company, 1965, p. 168.

5. Caswell and Associates, <u>op</u>. <u>cit</u>., p. 72.

6. Solomon Abrams. "Principles of Human Relations in Curriculum Improvement," Unpublished doctoral dissertation, University of Pittsburgh, 1952, p. 258.

of teachers, principals, or other personnel, working cooperatively.

This principle, expressed almost universally by writers in the field of curriculum development, is the converse of the method used at the turn of the century, when a specialist was directed to write a course of study.

Working groups should consist of personnel who are invited and who want to work on the problem. A permissive experimental atmosphere must exist if the guide is to reflect the committee's best efforts.

All who are concerned with the program should have a chance to participate in the process to some degree. However, "there is a greater chance for success when smaller groups are used," as pointed out by the Metropolitan School Study Council.[7]

Guideline 5. All who are concerned with the program should have a part in the group planning.

Writers on curriculum development state that as many teachers as possible should participate, because such involvement will give teachers a stake and an interest in curriculum change, will strengthen the movement toward change, and will eventuate on to changed classroom practices.

But too large a group is unwieldy. According to Nault[8] and others, even though the teacher does not contribute an idea, he usually feels that he is involved if he has been invited to make suggestions, and may therefore be inclined to accept it.

Some writers advise that the entire community--the school staff, lay citizens, and pupils--should assist in determining the nature of the curriculum, each according to background and qualifications. Yet as Krug says, "profes-

---

7. Metropolitan School Study Council. Better High Schools Faster. Second report. New York: the Council, 1955, p. 3.

8. William H. Nault, "Can Curriculum Guides Be Effective?" Educational Leadership (April, 1955), pp. 410-414.

sional educators have rendered special training for their work and may legitimately be expected to contribute more than might be possible for other citizens."[9]

While pupils could not be expected to participate in curriculum planning as experts, they should have opportunities to affect the curriculum--they can advise from the standpoint of the learner.

Guideline 6. _Activity should be at the local level_.

Curriculum changes may be planned by the curriculum committee, but must be tested in classrooms. Conversely, the committee responsible for planning must develop ways of discovering and using ideas that have originated or have been developed in classrooms.

Curriculum planning must be ultimately related to classroom practices. The teacher must be placed in the center of improvement program, because the curriculum, although planned centrally, is never fully determined until the pupils have appeared in the classrooms. As Anderson says, "The teacher is the most important of the curriculum makers."[10]

Guideline 7. _Experimentation should be done by teachers_.

Without ideas from teachers in the school system, the curriculum would tend to become barren. According to Douglas, Bent, and Boardman:

Many teachers attempt innovations in their teaching methods, trying new techniques and services in the endeavor to find one which will bring more satisfactory results. This tendency opens to supervisors the opportunity to introduce the experimental methods as a means of assisting teachers to try out new practices or procedures under controlled conditions. . . .[11]

---

9. Edward A. Krug. _Curriculum Planning_. New York: Harper & Row, Publishers, Inc., 1957, p. 14.

10. Anderson, _op_. _cit_., p. 56.

11. Harl R. Douglas, Rudyard K. Bent, and Charles W. Boardman. _Democratic Supervision in Secondary Schools_. Boston: Houghton Mifflin Company, 1961, p. 163.

Guideline 8. _Use should be made of the best practices in effect locally and elsewhere._

The curriculum should be based on both theory and practice. Furthermore, it should be based on practices that have been successful locally. As is stated in the 1953 Yearbook of the American Association of School Administrators, "Findings of scientific research should be respected and incorporated into curriculum plans."[12]

However, this cannot be done blindly. The results of such research must be tried locally to see whether they are workable in the local situation.

For, as Abrams says, "The curriculum . . . will not be transplanted successfully from one school system to another."[13]

Guideline 9. _Channels of communication should be maintained and used._

The effectiveness of the cooperative group process of curriculum development depends on how closely the central planning group relates to the entire group of teachers who will use the curriculum. Communication between them must be a two-way affair. As Abrams recommends: "Effective communication will be established between individuals, between individuals and groups, and between groups engaged in committee work."[14]

The committee must be acquainted with local experimentation and with the best practices in effect locally. Conversely, Abrams suggests that, in order to let teachers know of progress being made. "The groups will keep records and will publish summaries of meetings."[15]

Guideline 10. _The new curriculum should be introduced_

---

12. American Association of School Administrators. _American School Curriculum_. Thirty-first Yearbook. Washington, D.C.: the Association, 1953, p. 82.

13. Abrams, _op_. _cit_., p. 45.

14. _Ibid_., p. 170.

15. _Ibid_., p. 171.

gradually, if teachers are to feel reasonably secure.

The new curriculum should be introduced to teachers, little by little, as it is being developed. It is brought to the attention of teachers through the use of various communication media. Every issue of a news letter, every bulletin, every teachers' meeting, every statement about the new guide helps to prepare teachers for it.

Even after the new curriculum is ready, its introduction into classrooms should continue to be gradual. As Alberty says, "The 'new curriculum' is not something that is 'installed' completely at a given time, but rather is put into effect as decisions are made and as conditions as to staff and resources can be worked out."[16]

The security of teachers must be considered in the introduction of new courses. Teachers' individual growth rates should be considered, and the new curriculum should be installed in each classroom when the teacher in that classroom is ready for it. However, there is a reciprocal responsibility on all supervisory and teaching personnel for putting into effect the new course as early as is feasible.

Guideline 11. Changing of the curriculum must be accomplished by changing the values, skills, and/or understandings of teachers through an educational program.

The curriculum is dependent upon what happens in classrooms. If the curriculum is to be changed, the activities in the classrooms must be changed. If these activities are to be changed, teachers must be changed. As Evans states, "The notion that changing the curriculum means changing people has apparently taken firm root in the thinking of educators."[17]

As has been stated previously, the primary means of changing teachers is through participation in the changing

---

16. Harold Alberty. Reorganizing the High School Curriculum. New York: The Macmillan Company, 1953, p. 442.

17. Hubert M. Evans, "Organization for Curriculum Development," Review of Educational Research, Vol. 27, No. 3 (June, 1957), p. 287.

of the curriculum.

Guideline 12. Many means of curriculum improvement should be used.

A well-planned in-service education program should be a part of curriculum development. In fact as Hugh B. Wood observed: "Curriculum improvement as a process has become synonymous with supervision and in-service education, for many techniques have grown out of good supervisory practices and in-service training."[18]

Thus, curriculum improvement is seen to be dependent upon in-service education which may utilize many means. Abrams concurs as he says, "The procedures will stimulate the use of many varied means of improvement including: action research clinics, in-service courses, surveys, cooperative studies, and workshops."[19]

Guideline 13. Evaluation of the process of curriculum development should be made continuously.

The process of curriculum improvement is viewed as change in human relationship and this is affected by changing group relationships.

As Abrams says, "The organization will be continuously evaluated to determine its effect on the improvement of human relations, and its contribution to the establishment and maintenance of the requisite healthy conditions for the improvement of the curriculum."[20]

It therefore becomes the function of the administration and the curriculum group to evaluate the process being used, the material being introduced, and the teachers for whom the course is being developed. Changes in the process must then be made in the light of evaluation.

---

18. In: A. Harry Passow, "Organization and Procedures for Curriculum Improvement," Review of Educational Research, Vol. 24, No. 3 (June, 1954), p. 227.

19. Ibid., p. 262.

20. Ibid.

Guideline 14. Curriculum revision should be a continuous process.

The organization for curriculum development should not pass out of existence when the new curriculum is ready. The work should be continuous, rather than sporadic. As Caswell and Campbell state, "A course of study should be mimeographed, rather than printed, until it has been through several revisions."[21]

Although the process of mimeographing is not the essential point, the statement does emphasize that the publication be temporary in nature. During the early stages of the new course, teachers should try it out in pilot studies organized for that purpose. Suggestions should then be submitted to the curriculum committee so that the revision will incorporate the best thinking of all teachers.

As soon as the revised course is completed, evaluation is begun in the classrooms, and another cycle is started.

Although the superiority of one method of curriculum development over another probably cannot be shown experimentally, there is consensus that the cooperative group method of curriculum development is the best method. Certain procedural guidelines noted above have been agreed upon by writers in the field.

---

21. Hollis L. Caswell and Doak S. Campbell. Curriculum Development. New York: American Book Company, 1935, p. 9.

STAFF INVOLVEMENT: KEY TO CURRICULUM IMPROVEMENT

Richard G. Telfer

Consultant in Secondary Education
Colorado Department of Education
Denver, Colorado

Staff involvement is essential if curriculum improvement is to become a reality. The school administrator who fails to recognize this concept will in fact fail to provide the instructional program to meet the challenge of the changing social, political, and economic order of modern times. Daily, school leaders face problems for which they must find answers or provide solutions. These problems may include developing an in-service education program for their building, selecting new text materials, or charting the courses of the social studies program.

The alert administrator realizes that, within his building or system, he has a wealth of resources--his staff members. The task then becomes one of involving the faculty in developing solutions for these problems. Some of the group will be willing to help regardless of the situation. Some will have no desire to participate, but have much to offer as resource persons. The challenge as seen by the administrator is: "How will I secure the help and cooperation of the entire staff on a project for which I have the basic responsibility?"

Reprinted by permission from Clearing House, Vol. 43 (May, 1969), pp. 539-542.

There are certain basic facts that the administrator either knows of or should know about his staff. He should know their strengths and weaknesses in their subject field. He should know their ability to work cooperatively with other staff members. He should know their attitude toward participation in building or system projects. He should know the techniques necessary to stimulate action on the part of each member or groups of members.

The problem of involving the staff in curriculum improvement activities is made easier because of the fact that adults generally are attracted to groups or group activities. People like to have membership and obtain recognition in a group. This fact is easily observable if we just look around us at the many groups and organizations that exist in our society.

People become members of groups for many reasons. Verner and Newberry present evidence that people are joiners and like to participate in all types of activities, many for the purpose of improving a situation or their own proficiencies.[1] In observing schools where curriculum improvement is in evidence, one finds the action of groups. Throughout the country there is increased emphasis on the concept of staff participation for curriculum study and improvement. Gibbons indicates the need for involving all persons affected by an educational change. He believes that all should work, study, and plan together if the change is to be understood and accepted.[2]

The extent to which such participation will be meaningful is largely dependent upon the degree to which the participants will contribute to the group and to what extent their individual needs are met or challenged.

---

1. Coolie Verner and John S. Newberry, Jr., "Nature of Adult Participation," Adult Education, Vol. 8, No. 4 (Summer, 1958), pp. 208-222.

2. Charles Gibbons, "Improving the Climate for Creativity in Your Organizations," Advanced Management Journal, Vol. 19 (July, 1964), pp. 43-49.

Dobb discovered that men strive harder as they perceive better and that they perceive better the more they become involved in a situation.[3] This evidence gives strength to the need for allowing people to become involved in formulating plans or programs which will affect their work.

Many school administrators have found it advantageous to allow the staff to participate in decision making in an area such as curriculum improvement. The wise administrator does not give a directive to the staff regarding a pending curriculum study, but rather extends an invitation to them.

The instance to be cited is typical of many taking place throughout the country each year.

A newly appointed director of instruction of a district found resistance on the part of the faculty to accept materials that had been administratively developed in the "front office," without consideration of pupil or faculty needs, and had been issued with the statement, "This is to be followed to the letter." Needless to say no amount of coaxing could bring about its use.

Through observation of the problem it was evident that there was a need for assistance in the science area and that there were many teachers doing a fine job in certain science areas.

The following approach was attempted with productive results. A meeting of the faculty involved with the teaching of science was called. Coffee and rolls were served during the informal discussion period. Action began in a positive way. "During my visits to your classrooms I have noted, with interest, the many fine activities going on in the science areas. Some of you have indicated an interest in getting more usable ideas to help your pupils. All of you have said that the resource guide prepared two years ago does not meet your needs. What suggestions do you have for improving

---

3. Stuart Dobb, "Conditions for Motivating Men," Journal of Personality (June, 1957), pp. 489-594.

our science instruction?" Immediately several teachers suggested the formation of a curriculum committee for the study of the science problems. Within minutes a committee of volunteers was formed.

The results of this committee's work and study was a teacher developed resource guide which has been used extensively by the teachers. An improvement in science instruction was also evidence as a result of teacher participation in the setting of goals for the program. Here the role of the director was not that of dominator but rather that of a stimulator and resource consultant. The responsibility for the total instructional program had not been relinquished; rather, by placing the task in the hands of the faculty, the director's work was made easier and the program was accepted.

The technique just presented is not unique for any one system but is used throughout the country by school systems where real action is desired. Faculty members are basically engaged in creative work and want to develop their own materials.

Research conducted by Roman further supports this concept. Roman found that professionals engaged in mentally creative work became more effective when the responsibility for goal setting was shifted to them from their superiors.[4]

Additional support for the concept of nonadministrative domination of meetings and activities is found in a study done by Blumberg and Amidon. The two types of faculty meetings were studied: principal centered and faculty centered. The results of the study indicated that teachers were more willing to participate in the teacher centered type of meeting and that they felt better about their work as a result of the participation.[5]

---

4. Daniel Roman, "Project Management Recognize R & D Performance," Academy of Management Journal, Vol. 7 (March, 1964), pp. 7-20.

5. A. Blumberg and E. Amidon, "Teacher Reaction to School Faculty Meetings," Journal of Educational Research (May-June, 1963), pp. 466-470.

Unfortunately, all administrators have not realized the potential of the productive capacity of their faculties. Such administrators have been heard to say, "My staff just doesn't want to do anything with regard to participating in curriculum improvement activities." In an attempt to determine the validity of such a statement, a survey designed to determine the willingness of teachers to take part in planning staff meetings, setting course goals, and serving on curriculum study committees was given to 70 teachers enrolled in an education workshop at Wayne State University.

Results of the Study

Question I

As an educator do you welcome the opportunity to become involved in setting goals, serving on productive committees, and helping in planning meetings?

Yes 91% No 7% Sometimes 2%

Question II

Does your principal give you an opportunity to participate or become involved in setting goals, planning meetings, and serving on committees?

Yes 70% No 26% Sometimes 4%

Of those who were not given a chance to participate, 88% would have welcomed the opportunity, while 12% of the group didn't want to participate.

Though the sampling is limited, it does give an indication of how teachers feel about becoming involved in matters which will directly affect their work. Administrators such as the one quoted earlier should withhold comment regarding the willingness of their faculty to participate until they have evaluated their own values, objectives, and techniques. It would seem safe to say that teachers, if given proper opportunity, welcome the chance to become involved with goal setting, meeting planning, and committee membership.

In addition, each teacher surveyed was asked to rate certain professional competencies of school administrators.

Competency	Essential	Desirable	Not Necessary
Ability to motivate others	70%	30%	--
Can delegate	63%	35%	2%
Can maintain leadership without dominance	71%	29%	--

It would seem reasonable to conclude that teacher interest in having administrators with these qualities is a further indication of their desire to participate in school affairs.

In attempting to determine effective techniques used by administrators for involving their faculties in curriculum improvement projects, some 20 representative administrators most frequently mentioned included such activities as workshops, weekly staff meetings, round table conferences, problem solving situations, role playing, and even the suggestion box.

Each of the techniques suggested is basically designed to stimulate program improvement and teacher acceptance of a particular program. Administrators who use such techniques have recognized that there is little professional growth on the part of a faculty member who never receives recognition of his ideas or never becomes a participant in curriculum improvement activity.

There seems to be adequate evidence to support the basic premise that people, and in this case teachers, like to become involved in goal setting, decision making, and planning type activities. The administrator who capitalizes on this fact by providing situations that allow his faculty to become involved in these processes has recognized the motivational technique that will stimulate his faculty to a productive end.

IN-SERVICE EDUCATION: BALANCE AND THRUST

Leslee J. Bishop

Executive Secretary
ASCD

For years now, the pressure has been on to experiment, to innovate, to adapt and implement. While the rate of change has not pleased the impatient, many significant modifications have occurred or are in the wings awaiting their cue.

The early curriculum packages that were developed avoided in many cases the participants who should have been most involved--teachers, pupils, principals and supervisors. These were the days of the "teacher-proof" developments. Innovative imports tended to become curriculum dropouts because without in-service support and teacher commitment there were inadequate forces to continue.

Hardware was brought without an adequate support system of resources and personnel. Also, in too many cases, there was too little effort to assist teachers to develop the significant and necessary competency to manage the import. Without special funding the mortality rate ran high. Often the innovation that sold a school quickly became a requirement, a feature of that school and one that the patrons and professionals felt obliged to maintain, to build in, to rigidify. This meant that it lost its newness, its flexibility, the possibility of change and the necessary objectivity for evaluation.

Reprinted by permission from _Educational Leadership_, Vol. 25 (October, 1967), pp. 10-11.

Decision making in curriculum matters is changing rapidly. Improvements are likely to be imported from outside the system. They are likely to result from adaptation, not from "scratch." They may come in the form of reconsidered concepts in a discipline that are developed by scholars in the field, psychologists, teachers, and curriculum consultants; they may come as media or as organizationally induced changes that significantly modify the learning situation; they may come as packages of content, procedures, media evaluation; they may come as political imperatives that penetrate to the heart of the learning enterprise. In any case, more and more curriculum decisions are larger, more complex, more expensive, more consequential and require more significant teacher modification in the package and in the performance of both the teacher and the learner.

It has been suggested as a procedural consideration that the cost of an improvement should at least be matched by educational reinforcement and commitment at the local level. Curriculum that is behaving and dynamic requires new and special skills, new resources and materials, new perceptions regarding student and teacher roles and supervisory support, both in terms of leadership and continuing understanding and support.

The Growing Edge

Virtually every new curricular modification requires new teaching and learning strategies. These have been important ingredients of the new developments. Most of the methods required run contrary to the experiencing of the teacher, and most have not had adequate treatment in the development of the new curriculum scheme. Discovery, inductive teaching, inquiry, student generalizing and the rest are both critical to the success of the new developments and fragile in their own right. New procedures are needed for student evaluation, for teacher evaluation and even for the routines that surround the classroom enterprise at all levels. Without classroom resources, building modifications and supervisory support, most of the new endeavors in curriculum cannot culminate in effective student behavior.

Teacher militancy and the spreading effects of the negotiation process will seriously modify the procedures and patterns for in-service education. Teachers are insisting that they be considered full-fledged members of the educational team. They are seeking to revise and in some cases upset the traditional hierarchies of supervision and administration to the effect that these persons become supportive rather than directive. This is not a textbook revolution but a real change in the way supervisory and administrative staffs are perceived and will affect the ways in which they can and must operate. It is not the function of supervision to change people; it is very much its function to help people to change in ways that will make their performance more professional, more effective and more enhancing of the curriculum objectives and the goals of the school as an enterprise in society.

The support system must not only be more effective, it must be collegial in nature. It must not only include knowledge of what is new and better, it must also include means to improvement and support for that development.

The most significant changes will result from the improvements in teacher perceptions, in commitments and in competencies. As these affect the classroom situation, we are back to the crux of the matter for which the improvement was instituted. We have been prodded by sources to change. To make the changes effective for learners and teachers is the responsibility of the profession. These changes in fact become the significant element in innovation and curriculum improvement. It is at this point that in-service education represents not an adaptation of an outside product, but the creation of a significantly improved development within a system and within the classroom. This thrust is indeed a needed one and should be viewed as a significant function in the present concern for improvements in education. Just as evaluation should be used for feedback and guide, so in-service education should be used for adaptation and innovations.

SUPERVISORY ROLES OF ELEMENTARY PRINCIPALS

Fred Snyder

Assistant Professor of Education
Indiana State University

The elementary principalship is not only the oldest but one of the most essential administrative and supervisory positions in our public schools. Colonial schools had a head teacher or principal whose responsibility was to teach. As schools grew, the principal was given administrative duties. Thus, the role of the principal was created.

It has always been difficult to distinguish between the administrative and supervisory roles of elementary principals. For purposes of this writing, the supervisory roles of the principal will be considered as the activities pursued by the principal which are directly related to the improvement of teaching.

Frequently, the roles of the principal are perceived in terms of extremes on a time continuum. Many perceive the principalship as it has been in the past. They look upon the roles of the principal as pertaining to office routine, discipline, and arbitrary authoritative leadership. Others think of the principal as being one who presently lives in conditions of the future. These individuals see the principal as functioning in an atmosphere of democratic leadership and professionality. The fact is that neither of these two extremes is true. Certainly we have come a long way from

---

Reprinted by permission from Contemporary Education, Vol. XXXIX (May, 1968), pp. 274-275.

considering the principal as just an evaluator of teachers, but we are only on the threshold of many innovations which will affect the role of the principal.

Forward-looking elementary principals recognize that their present role is everchanging. They know that this role includes providing true leadership for the consideration and implementation of such innovations as team teaching, independent study, large-group instruction, small-group discussion, flexible organization, use of para-professionals, and a greater use of technical aids to teaching.

One prerequisite to implementing any innovation in an elementary school program is sound supervisory practices on the part of the principal. Such supervisory responsibility begins with a good program of teacher orientation. Not only do teachers new to the school need orientation assistance, but review of the school philosophy, procedures, and practices is necessary for all teachers from time to time. The wise principal considers orientation of teachers to be a continuous program which dovetails with his role of assisting teachers in providing better instruction. In both these roles, the principal functions as a co-worker helping the teachers to meet the needs of their learners.

The present trend is for superintendents to concentrate their time and efforts on community aspects of the school system. This trend has placed more importance on the supervisory role of the elementary principal. This role includes evaluation and possible revision of philosophy, methods, and curriculum content. The goal of the principal's evaluation is maintaining a good educational program which meets the individual needs of all students.

There are at least four explicit dimensions directly related to the supervisory role of the elementary school principals: (1) instructional staff rapport, (2) conferences with teachers, (3) in-service educational programs, and (4) association with students.

Teacher rapport which is related to mutual respect and appreciation can best be accomplished when the principal functions as a co-worker dedicated to the welfare of the students. Such a role involves frequent contact with children in the classroom, not as a visitor, or evaluator, but as an individual who is helpful to both teacher and students. Teacher rapport requires knowledge of the on-going program of learning and problems related thereto. It is a result of friendly assistance in which the principal maintains his leadership role, but functions as a participant sharing his knowledge and experiences for improved teaching and learning.

Conferring with teachers includes both individual and group conferences at appropriate times. It is reasonable to assume that one prerequisite to improvement of teaching is open two-way communication. It is much more than simply making announcements via the intercom system. It is more than discussing evident problems with teachers. Principal-teacher communication should be considered as a basic avenue for the prevention of problems. The individual conferences should be conducive to the offering of suggestions by both principal and teacher. Group conferences should be directed toward topics which are of concern to all in attendance. The role of the principal in both individual and group conferences is one in which he serves not only as a spokesman but as a very good listener as well.

In-service educational programs pertain to the on-going program of curriculum and methodology of teaching study. Such programs must be based upon the needs and interests of staff members. One of the greatest problems facing elementary principals is finding time for continued education and study programs of staff members. Universities through summer and extension programs can provide a great deal of assistance, but cannot meet the total need. Each school is unique and study directed toward meeting the needs of staff members is important for each particular school. This fact necessitates cooperative planning between the principal and staff members to define in-service goals and to set aside time which can be devoted to this salient aspect of instructional improvement.

Student association is basic to principals' understanding of children's educational needs. It is only through knowing the children that the principal can hope to know the needs of the school. The school is not in the final analysis an association of professional educators; it is not merely a building, even though professional educators and modern educational plants are important. It is composed of children who in many ways are alike, yet each is different from the other. It is these likenesses and differences which the principal must recognize and understand if he is to provide the necessary leadership in his various supervisory roles.

In the present situation, particularly in large buildings with many stairs, or older "egg crate" buildings, many classrooms are isolated. Similar isolation of the teaching processes which take place in these rooms must be avoided. Supervision is not an invasion of the classroom teacher's privacy. The classroom by definition is not a private laboratory for the teacher. Obviously in each case there are always twenty-five or more "reporters" present, eager to expound on existing classroom conditions, undaunted by the inaccuracy of their reports. The elementary principal cannot adequately function in his supervisory role on the basis of limited secondary information from either teachers or pupils. He is not just a hallway pacer catching glimpes of classroom activity as he passes by open doors. He is not an office fixture commanding "his ship" by remote control. On the contrary, as supervisor, he is a colleague who functions best in the classroom where he can be most helpful and can provide the most service. He is concerned with maintaining staff rapport, sound practices of communication, better teaching, and improved learning. It is most important that the principal be aware that supervision is his major role. His success in this role can be evaluated only in terms of improved teaching and in greater opportunities for student learning.

GROUP SUPERVISION: A TECHNIQUE FOR IMPROVING TEACHING BEHAVIOR

Edmund J. Amidon

Associate Professor of Educational Psychology
College of Education
Temple University
Philadelphia, Pennsylvania

Kathleen M. Kies

Director of Personnel in the Lower Merion School District
King of Prussia, Pennsylvania

Anthony T. Palisi

Assistant Professor of Education
Seton Hall University
Orange, New Jersey

The principal-teacher conference which usually follows observation of an instructional period is often conducted with the air of confidentialness as the interview between doctor and patient or lawyer and client. This confidential approach to supervision, which has been widely promulgated and accepted, suggests that the discussion involves criticism of the teacher and that only he may profit from the interview. It suggests that the interview is concerned more with the teacher than with the act of teaching.

Reprinted by permission from National Elementary Principal, Vol. XLV (April, 1966), pp. 54-58.

While this approach to supervision has value and is necessary at times, the authors propose that a different kind of supervision is at least equally appropriate. If supervision, defined as THE IMPROVEMENT OF INSTRUCTION, can be carried out so that teachers perceive it as "challenge without threat," perhaps we can take another approach--an approach which directs attention to THE ACT OF TEACHING, rather than to the teacher.

In directing attention to the act of teaching, one might hypothesize that group supervision can be as effective as group counseling appears to be. One can also hypothesize that such a process is more economical of supervisory time and that the dynamics of small groups enhance both the effect of the process and interpersonal relationships among the faculty. Small group process almost invariably has these effects: (1) Communication is opened; (2) Cohesiveness is encouraged; (3) Group norms are clarified for general understanding; and (4) Group goals are clarified.

In attempting to explore the potential of group supervision, the authors felt it necessary to define the act of teaching. Combs and Snygg hold that the genius of good teaching lies in the ability to challenge students without threatening them and that the distinction between challenge and threat lies "not what the teacher THINKS he is doing, but in what the student perceives him to be doing."[1] Thus, the task is to study the act of teaching in terms of this ability to challenge without threatening, as perceived by students.

The communication between teachers and students is sometimes non-verbal; however, it is largely composed of verbal behavior, and by objectively observing this talk, one can analyze the teacher's ability to challenge without threat. The authors' concern is to increase teachers' sensitivity to their own verbal behavior and their understanding of how this

---

1. A. Combs and D. Snygg. <u>Individual Behavior</u>. Evanston: Harper and Row, 1961.

behavior affects classroom climate and individual pupils. The Flanders System of verbal interaction analysis provides the teacher with an instrument of objectivity through which he can compare his own performance with his intentions and study teacher-pupil dialogue.[2] This system was used as the basis for an in-service training program carried out by the authors.

The Flanders System

Flanders classifies classroom verbal interaction in ten categories, seven of which identify teacher talk. Categories 1, accepting and clarifying student feeling, 2, praising or encouraging student behavior, 3, accepting and clarifying student ideas, and 4, asking questions, are considered indirect teacher talk. Categories 5, lecturing and giving information or opinion, 6, giving directions, and 7, justifying teacher authority, are considered direct teacher talk. Student categories 8, response to the teacher, and 9, student initiated talk, classify student talk. Category 10 is used to identify silence or confusion.

The observer, who may be present in the classroom or who may listen to a tape, records in sequence every three seconds the appropriate category numbers. When the lesson is over, the observer enters the numbers in the form of tallies in a 10-row by 10-column grid called a matrix. The matrix reveals both quantification and patterns of verbal interaction.

Data which was related to quantification include the percentage of time consumed (1) by teacher talk, (2) by student talk, and (3) in silence or confusion. The percentages of time spent in each of the seven categories of teacher talk may be computed.

---

2. E. J. Amidon and N. Flanders, "The Effects of Direct and Indirect Teacher Influence on Dependent Prone Students Learning Geometry," Journal of Educational Psychology, Vol. 52 (1961), pp. 286-291.

The matrix, while summarizing the data found by the observer, also maintains some of the sequence. The teacher can see the patterns of his instructions to pupil response, to silence, or to student initiation. He may find answers to such questions as, "Which of my verbal behaviors seem to elicit student response?" and "At what point in the interaction do I find it necessary to criticize?"

The Flanders System of interaction analysis does yield descriptive information about the teacher-pupil dialogue, but this information is IN NO WAY an evaluation of teaching. If any kind of value judgment about teaching is to be made, it is done by the teacher himself after studying his own interaction patterns.

This system was developed and refined by Flanders in the early 1950's. The first research related to children's attitudes to patterns of teacher behavior. Results of the research indicated that pupils of teachers who were observed to be indirect had more positive attitudes toward the school, the teachers, and other pupils than did pupils of those teachers who were identified by observers as direct. This research supports the validity of interaction analysis as a tool for predicting general attitudes of children in a school classroom.

Several studies have been designed to relate pupil attitudes and pupil achievement to teacher behavior.[3] These studies, using interaction analysis, present supporting evidence for the following conclusion: above average achievement and positive student behavior appear to be related to certain kinds of teacher behavior such as acceptance and

---

3. Idem.

E. J. Amidon and M. Giammatteo. *The Verbal Behavior of Superior Teachers*. Philadelphia: Group Dynamics Center, Temple University, 1964.

N. A. Flanders. "Teacher Influence--Pupil Attitudes and Achievement." Final Report, U. S. Office of Education Cooperative Research Project No. 397. Minneapolis: University of Minnesota, 1960.

clarification of student ideas, use of direction and criticism, amount of time spent in talking, and the encouragement of student-initiated talk.

This research appears to have implications for teacher education, and studies have been conducted in which interaction analysis was taught as an observational tool to teachers or student teachers.[4] Findings of these studies indicate that interaction analysis does effect observable changes in teacher patterns of verbal behavior. After training, teachers were observed as: (1) more encouraging and accepting, (2) less critical, (3) more indirect, (4) more positive in their attitudes toward teaching, (5) more successful (by superior's rating) in student teaching, (6) talking less, (7) giving fewer directions, and (8) permitting more student-initiated talk. These are changes in the perception of teaching and attitudes toward teaching as well as in actual teaching behavior. The researchers cited believe that the major cause of the changes was training in interaction analysis.

The In-service Program

Unique in its simplicity, this system, nonetheless, does require study. To be able to interpret or to under-

---

4. N. A. Flanders. *Helping Teachers Change Their Behavior*. Ann Arbor: University of Michigan, 1962.

J. Hough and E. J. Amidon. "An Experiment in Pre-Service Teacher Education." Unpublished paper. Washington, D. C.: American Educational Research Association, NEA, February, 1964.

J. Kirk. "The Effects of Teaching the Minnesota System of Interaction Analysis on the Behavior of Student Teachers." Unpublished doctor's thesis. Philadelphia: Temple University, 1964.

R. D. Zahn. "The Effects of the Attitudes of Cooperating Teachers on Attitudes of Student Teachers." Unpublished paper. Glassboro, New Jersey: Glassboro State College, 1964.

stand the interpretation of a matrix, teachers need about ten to twelve hours of training. A two-year in-service program was initiated in an elementary school so that the staff might learn to use this tool to aid in studying their own teaching. The school staff consisted of twenty-two teachers, the principal, and seven part-time specialists. Approximately twenty persons participated in the training program which consumed five two-hour meetings, held at weekly intervals. The primary objective of the first year of the program was to enable staff members to interpret matrices of their own lessons. Training included tape listening for practice in categorization and construction of matrices and some interpretative discussion of the matrix.

At the conclusion of the first year of the program over half of the teachers decided to analyze their teaching through the analysis of verbal interaction. In the traditional-principal conference, these teachers were presented, without value judgment, matrices of their own teaching. Some of the teachers studied further and began to state objectives for particular lessons in terms of teaching patterns which they wished to develop.

At the end of the first year, the group discussion culminated with suggestions that students be given more time to frame answers to questions and that teachers give more attention to the phrasing of questions. This discussion clearly centered about the teacher-pupil dialogue and its application to supervision in a group setting. The teachers in the group were also concerned with problems which they perceived to be common to most group members. In this case, the teachers felt that recommendations ought to be given to the group as a whole rather than to any one individual. It is important to note, in this connection, that a distinction between "supervision in a group setting" and "group supervision" is made in this paper. The former is group emphasis on a problem seen as common to the group. The latter provides that "individuals explore and analyze their own problems" within a group. Focus on individual problems came during a second year, with the crystallization of the concept of group supervision and with a group analysis of tape recordings of their own teaching.

The ground rules accepted by the group established that feedback would be offered only in areas that were perceived as susceptible to change by the recipient if he so desired and that feedback would be in the form of observation rather than interpretation. At any time, any member of the group could request that the tape be stopped in order to raise questions or to offer feedback.

As each of the taped lessons was concluded, the interaction analysis data for the lesson were presented to the group for discussion. Coupling information about a teacher's interaction pattern with group feedback and his own objectives, the teacher was asked to analyze his teaching.

Some of the major concerns of the group were for: (1) communication among pupils, as well as communication between individual pupil and teacher; (2) the cuing behavior of teachers, as it affects pupil participation; (3) reflection of pupil ideas, as a powerful factor in influencing pupil participation; and (4) projection by teachers of their own reactions and feelings to children.

Some of the more important hypotheses developed by the teachers were those regarding the possible effect of interrupting a child, of anticipating student feelings, of questioning techniques, and of searching for a right answer in group discussions. They further designed in-class skill sessions for testing these hypotheses and experimented with behaviors which seemed to offer productivity.

Procedures and Ground Rules

As a result of the experience which the authors have had over a two-year period, several ideas have been developed which may be useful for those interested in doing this type of work with teachers.

The most important factor affecting climate of the group is the way in which members give feedback to one another about a tape recording which the group is auditing. A first step in setting up a successful group climate would seem to be the development of ground rules for giving feedback. The following rules were set up and used by the faculty group described in this article:

1. The person giving feedback describes, rather than evaluates, the pattern of teaching. He attempts to give as objective a description as possible of what he heard happening, and he avoids saying that it was good or bad.
2. Feedback is offered only in areas that are perceived as susceptible to change by the recipient. For example, there is really not much use in discussing a teacher's stuttering, since he may have no power to change this except through intensive therapy.
3. Feedback is given only upon request of the person whose teaching is being discussed. If a teacher is playing his tape and is interested in the group's reaction, observation, or perception, he will ask for feedback.
4. Feedback is concerned with those aspects of teacher behavior that are characteristic of the teacher at the time that discussion is taking place, rather than aspects of behavior that are characteristic of an earlier time. This is to say that material open to discussion should be current, not that of a previous year.
5. Feedback does not require a teacher to defend his personal opinion or feelings about the way in which he is teaching. Feedback should help to clarify in the light of how others see a particular segment of teaching, rather than try to seek reasons for holding a particular philosophy or a particular attitude toward the teaching act.

6. Feedback is concerned with specific teaching acts not with generalized interpretations. It can be concerned legitimately with the manner of questioning used, manner of responding to students, pace, or some other pattern of communication.

These ground rules were honored in the breach generally, and were invoked only when feedback was perceived as being threatening to the recipient.

The writers also were concerned about what seemed to be the most appropriate composition and size of the group. The group has to be large enough to include all of the skills necessary for its successful functioning and yet small enough to give each teacher an opportunity to become involved and to discuss his own teaching. A reasonable size may be somewhere between five and twelve members. The size also seems to depend upon the amount of time the faculty has available for the particular activity. Usually a staff using this process will want to adjust the size of the group to the amount of time available. Therefore, if a group has three hours a week, it might be appropriate to have ten to fourteen in the group. On the other hand, if the group has only one hour a week, a smaller size would seem to be indicated.

Techniques

The first and most important activity is that of using INTERACTION ANALYSIS to analyze one's own tape recording. Learning appears to be maximized if a teacher knows interaction analysis. Once he has learned it, he should be given the opportunity of classifying his own tape recording and also that of other teachers.

ROLE PLAYING is perhaps one of the most widely used tools for improving teacher behavior. There are a number of ways of using role playing in combination with tape listening and interaction analysis. One type of role playing experience which the writers found useful was to ask a teacher to produce only certain kinds of behavior in a teaching situation. He might try to ask only very broad questions or only very narrow questions. He might try to produce only praise statements in response to a student, only critical statements, or only direction-giving statements. The value of this technique is that it gives the teacher an opportunity to practice behaviors with which he may not be familiar and helps him to become more flexible in his behavioral repertoire. A secondary purpose is that it gives a teacher a chance to note the impact a particular kind of behavior is having on students. If a teacher becomes more critical than is his custom, he can see the impact of criticism on his students.

Role playing can be conducted in the group while a tape recording is playing; the tape can be stopped at a given point, and the principal can inquire, "How else could the teacher have asked that question?," and then teachers can role play different kinds of questions. Or, the tape recording can be stopped as the teacher responds to a student, and the principal can ask, "How else could the teacher have responded to the student?" Again, teachers will have an opportunity to role play various kinds of reactions. Role playing can also be done in the classroom after a teacher has been able to decide some of the things he would like to try. He can plan some teaching patterns he would like to try, go into his classroom and role play them, and tape the lesson in order to provide himself with feedback. While he listens to his tape, he will have some indication of the extent to which he has been successful in achieving the pattern he intended.

TAPE RECORDING, in general, is perhaps the most under-used teacher training technique. It is under-used in the sense that teachers seldom listen to their own performances. Yet the machine is simple to operate, it is usually available, and it provides immediate and live feedback for the teacher. Simple tape listening, with the group, has a major focus for the use of interaction analysis in this group supervision. Our procedure has been to play tapes of various teachers, with the option available to all group members of stopping the tape at any time to discuss a point. Sometimes a more careful analysis of a given portion of the tape will be the outcome. Another use of tape listening is to play tapes other than those of the participants as examples of various teaching styles, so that the group may observe the differing results when the same lesson is taught in different ways. Obviously, it will be easily observed that there are many ways in which to teach the same lesson, and that there is no "right" way.

For changing behavior, one of the essential requirements is the process of DEVELOPING HYPOTHESES. In the group, teachers have started out by listening to a tape and discussing it, analyzing a matrix, and then proceeded to the development of questions about certain aspects of the interaction pattern. These questions are concerned with the change that a teacher might decide to make in his interaction pattern.

One of the most exciting activities in which teachers can engage is simply experimenting with teaching behavior. Although similar in one way to the developing of hypotheses, this activity often leads to creative teaching, thus, broadening the teachers' behavioral repertoire and helping them develop a truly experimental attitude.

Summary

It would appear that group supervision does provide some advantages that may be precluded in the traditional principal-teacher conference, particularly when confidentiality is not a requisite.

The authors believe that teachers did become sensitized to verbal interaction much as described in the cited research, and that the effect of group activity appeared to influence positively faculty interpersonal relationships, communications, goal-setting, and behavioral norms.

While group supervision may need to undergo the scrutiny of empirical research to provide data about the hypotheses advanced, the process appears to merit consideration.

IS IT REALLY NECESSARY FOR PRINCIPALS TO VISIT CLASSROOMS?

Carmen W. Lucas

Public Schools
Milwaukee, Wisconsin

Standards and qualifications for teaching have risen at a phenomenal rate since 1945, and they will continue upward. In the near future when our elementary schools become staffed with teachers who are specialists in their field and have earned graduate degrees in these fields, it will be difficult, if not impossible, for the principal to know as much as teachers about their areas of proficiency. The principal will not be qualified in most respects to advise or evaluate teachers. Or will he?

The good principal has always been an instructional leader, a master teacher. He has always refused to be shackled with administrivia. Yet voices are being raised today to inform us that elementary-school faculties of the next decade will be so highly specialized that a principal will not be competent to advise his teachers on instructional matters.

Every principal would enjoy being in a Utopian situation. But we have to face facts. One hard fact is that most elementary schools have two troublesome problems involving the teaching staff.

The first problem: new teachers coming out of colleges

Reprinted by permission from Elementary School Journal, Vol. 66 (February, 1966), pp. 245-248.

and universities are well versed in subject matter, but far too often have not been prepared to teach it to the child whose frustrations, arising from the problems of urban life, often cause him to be disturbed. Many children coming to school today are not trained in courtesy, obedience, and respect as they were in the past. This is evident not just in school but also in public places everywhere. The recent riots and demonstrations in some of our large cities are going to make the work of teachers much more difficult. The teacher may be highly specialized in his field and extremely learned, but if he cannot motivate pupils to want to listen and learn, he will fail as a teacher unless his principal can organize ways to help him. I am writing from years of observation.

The second problem: our career teachers of the past three or four decades are now retiring from the teaching profession, and many of the young teachers coming in as replacements do not stay in the profession long enough to learn the art and the science of getting across understandings to their pupils. This is especially true in the elementary schools. In times past, our schools were staffed with teachers who made teaching a career, but such schools are now rare. Many young women are entering our profession, but most of them leave within three years to marry and raise a family of their own. We might as well tell the public the truth. The turnover among teachers in elementary schools is creating a problem of great instability on school faculties. Just about the time supervisors and principals have teachers well trained in how to motivate and teach their pupils, these young teachers leave teaching for one reason or another. Teacher personnel departments tell us that if they did not hire these potentially transitory teachers, many of our classrooms would not have teachers. To help these teachers many principals have had to organize in-service programs that continue from year to year.

Principals would like to have a staff of teachers they did not have to worry about--teachers who were not only specialists in their subject area but were also skilled and experienced in motivating children to want to learn. In most elementary schools, however, this situation just does not exist and will not exist in the foreseeable future unless somehow the profession attracts more dedicated career teachers. In too many schools, we have a "teach until" situation.

We must not make the mistake of thinking that our teachers do not need help. Outside of the large-city systems that have a well-developed corps of curriculum supervisors, principals have to train teachers even though the new teachers have a five-year degree.

It is the principal's responsibility to see that his teachers are well prepared to give individual guidance and counsel. It is also the principal's responsibility to see that class size is kept small so that each teacher can use the efficacious, personal approach. Our schools should give our young people the warmth of security. Each child needs special attention from his teachers. Young teachers need help with this personalized approach.

One hallmark of a good teacher is alertness to recognize when pupils are and are not ready to learn. One hallmark of a good principal is alertness to sense when a teacher needs assistance. The good principal has the experience and the know-how to help and advise. A principal need not be an authority in a teacher's subject field. Even a teacher who is a specialist may need to be encouraged and evaluated on his presentation of material. Good teachers will always welcome classroom visits from their principal if they receive constructive comments from him on their teaching methods and the atmosphere of their classroom. Teachers who are having difficulty certainly need such help. Often they do not realize that they need help with their teaching procedures and classroom management.

Another responsibility a principal has is to be sure that his teachers have a plan for achieving the task they wish to accomplish. And he has the responsibility of protecting his teachers from interference so that they will have the freedom to carry out their plan. We emphasize the fact that children should experience success. Teachers, too, need success. A principal must be watchful of the well-being of his faculty and the pupils of his school. This requires classroom visits to ascertain the classroom climate and to determine whether the teacher needs help in attaining his teaching goals.

A principal should not visit the classroom to make direct criticism, but to join the group being taught and, if possible, to commend some phase of the work of the class and let the pupils know that he is interested in what they are studying. If the teacher needs helpful suggestions, they can be given later in private conference. It means much to a teacher, whether he is a specialist or a beginner, to know that every time the principal steps into the classroom a friend is coming in to help and support.

In the organization of a school, the principal can do much to help teachers achieve their teaching goals. The teaching schedule should not be rigid. Teachers should not be held to split second adherence to time allotments--so many minutes a day for this subject and so many minutes for that. Teachers should be permitted some flexibility in their schedule. In socialized discussion nothing is more disheartening than to have to bring to an abrupt close a stimulating discussion that, given a few more minutes, might have led to an important conclusion.

As the principal organizes his school, he should eliminate as many interruptions as possible and thus let teachers teach. Announcements and notices should be kept to a minimum and given at a certain time each day. The principal should free teachers from the pressure of being constantly on the lookout for the safety of their pupils. A pupil patrol can help with safety problems. The principal should never insist that teachers adopt a new technique of teaching until they are reasonably certain of having success with it.

A program of classroom visits can do much to improve

the teachers' effectiveness and the learning climate. The program should be wisely and humanely carried out. Pupils should know that their principal is interested in them, knows them, and cares about them. This knowledge gives them an added feeling of security and improves their attitude toward school and their studies. The pupils should be able to sense that their principal is understanding, sympathetic, considerate, and fair. One of the best ways the principal can make this known to them is to visit often in their classroom, to listen to their discussions, watch their demonstrations, and praise their achievements.

No elementary school should be so large that this cannot be done. Despite our mounting enrollments, we must not let our schools become so big that they are like production lines in huge, cold factories grinding out a product.

The principal must not permit himself to be relegated to his office as an administrator. He should be the inspirational and educational leader of his school for both teachers and pupils. They should look forward to his visits to their classrooms. Classroom visits by the principal can do much to help teachers help pupils achieve success in their learning. Classroom visits by the principal can do much to help teachers develop a sense of pride in their teaching and a desire to press on to new achievements and new accomplishments.

Let us face it, we cannot omit classroom visits and hope for the best. It is the principal's obligation to his pupils and their parents to see to it that they are getting the best. Classroom visits by the principal are really needed to help make this possible.

AN ANALYSIS OF INTERACTION AMONG PRINCIPALS AND TEACHERS DURING SCHOOL FACULTY MEETINGS

David B. Crispin

Associate Professor of Education
Indiana State University

and

Duane Peterson

Associate Professor of Education
Wayne State University, Michigan

Reporting their research on the attitudes of teachers toward faculty meetings, Blumberg and Amidon[1] write in the NASSP Bulletin: ". . . the critical variable accounting for differences in teacher attitudes from school to school seems to be the principal's behavior as reflected in the pattern of faculty meeting interaction . . ." and "more positive attitudes are associated with faculty-centered interaction (the locus of responsibility and control being with the faculty): more negative attitudes are related to principal-centered interaction (the locus of responsibility and control resting with the principal)." This pilot study aims to gather more information regarding principal-teacher

---

Reprinted by permission from Contemporary Education, Vol. 39 (May, 1968), pp. 287-290.

1. A. Blumberg and E. Amidon, "A Comparison of Teacher and Principal Attitudes Toward Faculty Meetings," The Bulletin, NASSP (March, 1964).

interaction during school faculty meetings. But where Blumberg and Amidon used the questionnaire method of data collection, the present study employs trained observers using interaction-analysis to observe and record the live behaviors of principals and teachers as they occur spontaneously during faculty meetings.

Blumberg and Amidon offer a useful conceptual dichotomy in which they classify principal-teacher interaction as either "principal centered" or "faculty centered," the difference being found in "the locus of responsibility and control." And this difference can be set forth in behavioral terms--when the principal behaves in such a way as to maintain responsibility and control, his behavior can be described as direct; when he behaves in such a way as to share the responsibility and control, his behavior can be described as indirect.

Teachers' behaviors can be dichotomized also, and in this study all teacher behavior is categorized as Supportive or Non-Supportive. While "behavior" and "attitude" have different meanings, this research accepts the assumption that attitudes are reflected in behavior; and it seems safe to generalize from Blumberg and Amidon's "positive" and "negative" attitudes to our definitions of Supportive and Non-Supportive behaviors respectively.

Blumberg and Amidon found more positive teacher attitudes associated with faculty-centered interaction. Expecting to find data supporting their findings, we used our operational concepts to restate their conclusion as our hypothesis.

Hypothesis: The more indirect the principal's behavior, the more supportive will be the teachers' behaviors.

Operational Definitions

Behavior: oral statements, and the manner in which statements are made, including tone of voice and facial expression.

Direct Behavior (principal): the principal uses his or the administration's position, ideas, or requirements; gives orders, directions, lectures; reads prepared directives or statements of policy; justifies his position or authority.

Indirect Behavior (principal): the principal willingly shares his authority with the teachers; shares and accepts both feelings and ideas; seems genuinely willing to be influenced by the teachers; encourages them to express themselves; aims for consensus.

Non-Supportive Behavior (teacher): the teacher seems to be participating only because he has to; he is defensive, uncooperative; he seems bored, inattentive, uninterested; he is perfunctory, seems to be behaving simply to get rid of the task.

Supportive Behavior (teacher): the teacher seems willingly cooperative; spontaneously, enthusiastically contributes feelings and ideas; he is attentively, seriously involved.

Independent Variable: the behavior of the principals.

Dependent Variable: the behavior of the teachers.

Controls: All faculty meetings were held after school and lasted 40-45 minutes. All principals and teachers discussed the topic "Utilization of Teacher Time." All the schools are elementary and are located in the Wabash Valley, Indiana. Faculty size ranged from five to twenty-three and averaged eleven (our data revealed no correlation between group size and either of the variables).

Procedures: Graduate students selected from a graduate course in interaction analysis at Indiana State University were trained intensively by the use of films and T-V tapes and live observing experiences until they achieved the level of .95 reliability in recording the categories. Behaviors were recorded sequentially as they occurred every three seconds or faster in case of change of speaker or behavior. Principals' behaviors were recorded with l's; teachers, with o's. Direct (principal) behaviors and Non-Supportive (teacher) behaviors were placed at the right of the column; Indirect (principal) and Supportive (teacher) behaviors, at the left. So that the record would not be distorted by a situation wherein one or two "supportive" teachers did most of the talking while the rest of the group was non-supportive, etc., a "G-factor" was recorded. "G" refers to group and is recorded as the observer's estimate of the supportiveness or non-supportiveness of the total group. When the G appears on the right of the column the observer found the group to be non-supportive; on the left, supportive. The days for the faculty meetings were randomly selected. When possible the observers were randomly assigned; however, the observers' class schedules determined their availability. When observers returned from a faculty meeting and presented their raw data, the meeting was discussed. For example, although the principals did use the topic "Utilization of Teacher Time," at some faculty meetings things occurred such as committee reports, and readings of minutes, and in one case even a brief birthday party; and such events were not included in the data for analysis. The raw data then resolved into I/D's and S/N's:

Principal behavior:

$$I/D = \frac{\text{Indirect}}{\text{Direct}}$$

so that the more indirect the principal's behavior the higher his I/D ratio.

Teachers' behaviors:

$$S/N = \frac{\text{Supportive}}{\text{Non-Supportive}}$$

so that the more supportive the teachers' behaviors the higher the S/N ratio.

G factors were also totaled and are reported as G-S when the group was supportive during half or more than half of the total interactions; and as G-N where the group was non-supportive half or more than half of the time. Therefore, the interaction can be analyzed in terms of our hypothesis, and if our hypothesis is supported by the data, we should find a high I/D accompanied by a high S/N and a Supportive G.

Findings: Our findings are set forth in Table 1.

Table 1

BEHAVIORS OF PRINCIPALS AND TEACHERS

Faculty Meeting	Principal's I/D (Ranked)	Teachers' S/N (Acts of Individuals)	Group (%)**
1	17.00	464.00	S-(100)
2	13.00	8.19	S-(71)
3*	10.18	51.33	S-(94)
4*	7.20	23.60	S-(90)
5	7.07	116.00	S-(99)
6	6.05	10.90	S-(81)
7	5.43	364.00	S-(100)
8	4.43	11.88	S-(93)
9	4.41	34.20	S-(97)
10*	3.79	67.33	S-(98)
11	3.62	438.00	S-(100)
12*	3.04	13.22	S-(92)
13	2.33	243.00	S-(100)
14*	2.09	516.00	S-(100)
15	1.53	18.75	S-(86)
16	1.32	37.20	S-(96)
17*	1.10	379.00	S-(100)
18*	.83	7.53	S-(80)
19	.77	30.00	S-(98)
20	.73	15.00	S-(83)
21	.59	161.00	S-(100)
22	.50	149.00	S-(100)
23	.49	19.20	S-(95)
24	.45	9.95	S-(88)
25	.39	203.00	S-(100)
26	.27	146.00	S-(97)
27	.25	2.55	N-(41)
28	.08	14.27	S-(86)
29	.08	3.00	S-(63)
30	.04	10.00	S-(100)

*Female
**% of total time group was Supportive

These data represent over 20,000 interactions among thirty principals and 311 teachers during thirty faculty meetings covering 1,350 minutes and they indicate that our hypothesis is rejected. There is no correlation between I/D's and S/N's these findings would occur by chance (r = .229--Pearson Product Moment Correlation Coefficient). According to our definition of supportiveness, these teachers were very supportive nearly all the time regardless of the directness or indirectness of the principals.

Of the nine faculty meetings evincing 100% supportiveness, five are above and four are below the median of principals' I/D's. Perhaps the most striking piece of evidence is that teachers behaved 100% supportively with both the principal with the highest I/D (17.00) and the principal with the lowest I/D (.04)!

In addition to the data discussed, we found other data relevant to our hypothesis; that is, the amount of participation by the teachers in the two different climates. The teachers who interacted with the principals whose patterns of behavior were indirect participated exactly twice as much as teachers in the direct climates. If we assign "direct climate" to those faculty meetings in which the principals' I/D's were 1.10 or lower, and "indirect climate" to those with I/D's higher than 1.10 we find:

Climate	Direct	Indirect
Average number of teacher behaviors	79	158

It is also interesting to note that of the thirty principals observed seven are females; and of the seven females, six behaved indirectly (I/D = 1.10 or higher) and the remaining one had an I/D of .83. Of course, this also means that the widest range of behavioral patterns was found among male principals. Our experience leads us to suggest that an I/D of 17 reveals an extremely indirect pattern, and an I/D of .04, an extremely direct pattern of behavior.

Conclusion: The evidence fathered in this pilot study suggests that the behaviors of teachers during faculty meetings are consistently supportive regardless of the directness or indirectness of the principal's behaviors. However, teachers participate more (twice as much) in the indirect climate.

Our findings are puzzling. Research findings in the areas of group dynamics, sociology and leadership, too numerous to mention, suggest that the behavior of the group is dependent upon the behavior of the leader (and this was revealed in our data regarding the amount of participation). How may we explain our findings, then? Two explanations seem reasonable: (1) observers cannot accurately categorize behavior, (2) teachers are mature enough to hide their feelings and not behave in ways likely to jeopardize their positions. After all, faculty meetings are recognized as part of a teacher's professional role and teachers are expected to behave "professionally" during faculty meetings. This implies that they might pretend to be interested, act as though they are concerned, even when they aren't. And perhaps this best explains our findings. Even if we allow that what our trained observers recorded as supportive behavior really wasn't supportive, whatever that behavior was and however it might be recorded, the fact remains that the behaviors of these teachers during these faculty meetings remained very much the same regardless of the behaviors of the principals which varied greatly. (As many as seven of these observations were done by the same person.)

In the article cited above, Blumberg and Amidon go on to say, "Generally, there is a very consistent trend for principals to perceive what transpires in their faculty meetings differently than do teachers." And later, "It may be precisely because of these attitudinal differences that principals and teachers experience some of the conflicts they do." Perhaps the findings of the present research shed new light on this "conflict" and "difference in perception" problem. Could it simply be that from the principal's point of view during faculty meetings it appears that the teachers are satisfied with the meeting? That they do seem to be behaving "supportively"? If they do seem to be supportive, and if their behaviors are not in keeping with their attitudes or feelings, surely here is a cause of the "conflict" and "difference in perception" reported by Blumberg and Amidon.

Implications for Further Research: Research should be designed to gather data regarding both the attitudes and the behaviors of both teachers and principals during faculty meetings. And it seems appropriate to use both interaction-analysis and post-session questionnaires.

Principals can be trained in interaction-analysis and many would be willing to try out different patterns of behavior during faculty meetings. The effects of different patterns of leadership upon the behaviors and attitudes of the teachers could be ascertained with interaction-analysis and questionnaires.

Research as suggested should be done in secondary schools and in larger urban schools. (This research was carried out in small elementary schools about half of which are in small towns and half in Terre Haute, Indiana, population 70,000.)

Copies of "The Crispin System of Interaction Analysis" may be obtained by writing to David Crispin, Associate Professor of Education, Department of Education and Psychology, Indiana State University, Terre Haute, Indiana 47809.

"OSMOSIS"--THE NEW SUPERVISION

William C. Jordan

Acting Superintendent
San Rafael Schools
San Rafael, California

If one reviews the college, graduate-level textbooks on organization, administration and supervision which have been published in the past 25 to 30 years, he will find that the major instrument of instructional change is a "committee." Almost without exception, author after author, the present writer included, points out that supervision, the improvement of instruction, is teacher oriented at the grass-roots level and that the "participatory process" is the one insurance policy that guarantees progress.

Invariably we administrators are told to gather about us a group of "interested teachers," define and delimit a problem, set up a hypothesis, attack the problem, determine alternatives, choose a solution and arrive(!) at a conclusion--be it a new method, report card, a new course of study, a recommendation about noontime supervision or adoption of a textbook. The advocates of this type of supervisory operation contend that the end product is not the important outcome but that the major contribution lies "in transit." The true goal, they say, is the intragroup, interpersonal relationships that mold teacher opinion as the group progresses, and teachers, seeing the reasons and need for revision, ac-

---

Reprinted by permission from Educational Leadership, Vol. 25 (October, 1967), pp. 54-61.

tually accept, for themselves, change which is put into action upon their return to the classroom.

Such committees, fortified by gallons of coffee--and possibly doughnuts--are clothed with such presently pertinent phrases as "democratic practices, involvement, communication systems, participation, group dynamics, feeling of belonging and purposeful activity." When you strip all the verbiage away, the educational administrator, supervisor or principal is saying, "We want the teachers to do what we want them to do, but, they must think it is their own idea!" Imagine! Another famous administrator indicates that he "gets teachers to do what he wants but entirely without friction"--again imagine!

One of the reasons that the educative process changes so slowly is that too many supervisors feel that teachers fall for this line of fluff. Teachers are not stupid! They are aware of the literature, they know that change is necessary; they patiently observe the rules of the game as played by some administrators and go stoically through the motions of meetings, and coffee and committee caravans as part of the price they must pay for membership in a fine and rewarding profession.

More deadly than the above questionable and limiting experience is the "group therapy" approach to supervision. Here we find the administrator-executive "curing" teachers by repealing the past. Little by little, step by step, he leads his staff out of the bloom of the professional profusion--as he sees it! This is the administrator who, in advance, knows what he wants, picks his own committee and tells it where he wants the group to go! And, what's more, gets there by leading his tethered teachers down the path of least resistance.

Again when one realizes that this process has been functioning for years under the cloak of democracy, one understands the lag of educational advancement. Teachers justifiably resent this type of nonsense as beneath their dignity. One will find thousands of courses of study, arrived at through such chicanery covered with dust, unnoticed by the teacher, in a stack on his desk or in his book cupboard. So much for "supervision" in its traditional form.

Let us now turn our attention to another chapter of progress. The words, "obligated boundary maintenance," should have special meaning to the supervisor who truly is interested in change. Obligated boundary maintenance indicates the reaction and resistance of a group to a suggestion of change. Even if the people (teachers) involved know that change is necessary, even though they know that new ideas, methods, materials or techniques are profitable, the group feels "obliged" to join hands and, with bowed heads, shout, "No!"

To change, you see, is tantamount to admitting that what one has been doing in the past is not "quite right"--and there are too few people in the world who are secure enough to admit that there might be a better way or that they are or have been wrong. We, all of us, therefore, deny progress by saying, "My kids are different; we did this before and it doesn't work; parents won't stand for it; my principal is against it; takes too much time" and on and on. There are hundreds of ways to scuttle a new idea.

A New Method

How, then, does one who wants to innovate, lead, create or simply supervise, organize for progress? The writer would like to offer a new method which for want of a better term I call "Osmosis," the gentle movement of liquid through a barrier.

To begin this "Osmosis" process, the supervisor-administrator searches through his own staff for teachers with adventurous souls. They are not hard to find. You take one teacher by the hand and say, "Come with me." With this one teacher, the supervisor works as a partner to develop a new teaching technique, explore a new method of organizing a classroom, experiment with a unique unit, build new methods of presentation of material or construct a continuing self-evaluation system for the students. One is limited here only by the ingenuity and creativity of the two educators involved.

While the "Osmosis" process is attractive and exciting, it should be obvious to any educational administrator that this operation can be "fraught." The process requires great delicacy; one must be extremely sensitive to the feelings of other teachers when a specific member of the staff may be given a surplus of notoriety and publicity. Professional jealousy is difficult to handle and administratively requires tact. We all know that the truly great teachers, the artists in the classroom, are usually dramatic classroom actors and the fact that someone else is a recipient of a great deal of applause and attention can breed dissatisfaction within the staff. It is obvious, then, that as the project goes on, the rest of the staff needs to feel secure. This is why the writer stresses continuously, "I like what you (the others) are doing, please don't change."

In essence the supervisor stops talking and starts doing. You quit telling teachers what and how they should be doing and start showing them. This is, then, the basic difference. Suddenly the supervisor becomes an enthusiastic partner in a teaching-learning situation. He becomes less a supervisor and more a co-worker in the vineyards of the profession. The management-labor aspect is completely eliminated as the leader leads because he earns it and deserves it through enthusiasm, drive and creative initiative, not because he is appointed. The difference of this "Osmosis" approach is, of course, quite obvious and from any standpoint pays premium dividends not only in improved instruction but what is more encouraging in improved staff morale.

There are only two criteria to be observed here: First, it must be fun for the teacher and the children, and second, it must be productive educationally.

When other teachers inquire about the new activity, you

say, "We're not sure the process works as yet." Every teacher, then, is positive he can make it work better! However, we are seldom in a hurry! To all teachers the writer says and means it, "You are wonderful just the way you are; you don't need to change; I like what you are doing right now. I could care less whether you change or not." When teachers feel that no one is trying to force them to change, no one is trying to slip something over on them, no one is going to "chew them out" for not changing, when they feel secure enough to try, they will try!

When the supervisor says, "Come with me, I will help you; I will show you," that one teacher will move forward confidently, secure in his or her guide. Moreover, when pressure and fear are removed and the pseudo-democratic drapery is eliminated, teachers move forward rapidly, happy at last to be treated as intelligent adults.

Change in Attitude

The writer had the opportunity and advantage of experimenting with this type of activity only briefly in the midwest, but has been able to bring the process to full fruition in San Rafael, California. Progress has been startling. On the wings of one or two exciting and excited teachers, ideas and techniques have spread through our small (225 teachers) school system with great rapidity.

However, and more important than the progress that has been made, is the change in attitude that one notices in teachers and administrators alike. Now that change is pleasant, it must be fun; and individual, no one is submerged in a group, ideas are springing from the staff with surprising and satisfying regularity. Not all of these ideas are productive but this is not important. What truly counts is the growing ability of some of our teachers, with such encouragement, to stand back from their activities and look at the total teaching-learning process with an objective professional eye, all the while saying, "Now, how can I do it better --or differently?"

As ideas pop up from the teachers and administrators we take them from school to school and teacher to teacher saying, "Who wants to take a look at this one?" It does not take long now, after two years, to find teachers who are anxious to share ideas, experiment, innovate. Now that invention is fun, nearly everyone wants to get into the process. We are at the point now at which, when we say, "Who wants to try to . . ." we seldom are able to finish the sentence. Everyone volunteers; no one wants to be left out. Teachers are saying "How come I didn't get to try that first?"

No one is naive enough to think that every individual teacher is wild about every idea or technique. Some teachers are always fearful of progress for the reasons already mentioned. Some will forever retreat into the past and sigh longingly for the good old days and for the "committee" operation wherein they can be submerged unnoticed in the group. This is not to be critical but to recognize people as they are. The height of absolute zero is a report card committee which after three years brings forth a report card that only half the staff approves when it is finally adopted.

While there is still a place, quite small in the writer's estimation, for a group meeting in education, the modern, dynamic professional leader will today find the "Osmosis" method (if given the right treatment) far superior to the traditional "committee and coffee caravan" of the past. We urge educational leaders to take off in high gear in a new direction with a new method. As a technique may we suggest "show" instead of "tell," individual instead of group, personal commitment instead of professional detachment as we work with teachers to lift "our" level of instruction. The results will be amazing!

BREATHE NEW LIFE INTO FACULTY MEETINGS

Anthony Saville

Assistant Professor
Bowling Green State University
Bowling Green, Ohio

A new teacher, reporting for work at 8:00 A.M. with several necessary tasks to complete before his 8:40 class, can be rather discouraged when he learns that a faculty meeting has been scheduled for 8:10 that morning!

Fifteen minutes later he is further demoralized when the principal merely reads the daily bulletin to the group, emphasizing some point which concerns only a small portion of the staff present. He quickly reaches the state of near-panic upon learning that these meetings (usually called without advance notice) are weekly affairs consisting of speeches and reports by the principal--a majority of which could have been included in a printed bulletin!

Certainly such administrative practices are not the rule; however, enough incidents of this nature have been reported to cause considerable concern among professional personnel.

Consequently, guidelines for organizing faculty meetings offered to provide direction for educational leaders unaware of the basic purposes of the general faculty meeting and as a review for those who have temporarily forgotten these basic principles. The primary purpose, however, is to

---

Reprinted by permission from Clearing House, Vol. 39 (September, 1964), pp. 40-42.

reassure teachers that these standards do exist and have existed in professional literature for some time. These guidelines also suggest how staff members could become more directly involved in planning and organizing general faculty meetings.

The primary aim of the general staff meeting is securing professional staff integration to augment better coordination of the entire educational program. This aim can be realized through the utilization of recognized objectives for general faculty meetings. These objectives include helping all teachers realize the variety of problems existing in their school; serving as a clearing house for ideas relating to some common problem; providing opportunities for vital committee, group, or individual reports of interest to all; reviewing studying, or initiating new procedures and techniques which might be utilized by the entire group, capitalizing upon and rewarding special skills; obtaining general staff reaction to specific situations; and improving group morale by providing a social atmosphere.

The following paragraphs are concerned with suggestions for planning and organizing such meetings.

1. The meetings should not consist of reports or statements that could have been placed in a special or daily bulletin. In fact, if these bulletins were originally well organized, meaningful, and well written, faculty members might, through habit and of respect, read them more carefully.
2. The general faculty meeting should be scheduled on an average of one per month-and-a-half, depending, of course, upon local school situations. This suggests, in effect, that a majority of the faculty gatherings should consist of smaller group sessions organized by subject areas, departments, grade levels, study groups, or other practical units, rather than numerous, poorly planned, administratively oriented large group meetings.

   In smaller schools with up to 15 staff members,

the small group is for all practical purposes synonymous with the entire staff. Even here, however, administrators, consultants, or supervisors have successfully divided their faculties into primary, intermediate, junior high (seventh and eighth grades), and sometimes subject area groups when dealing with specific curricular problems. Previously scheduled general staff meetings were then utilized to culminate common goals such as those discussed earlier in this article.

At the secondary level, department, subject area, or study area, or study group meetings should be utilized in dealing with problems in particular areas of concern to only a limited number of persons. Again, only the common issues should be treated in the general faculty meeting. These smaller groups or departmental meetings should be scheduled as frequently as necessary (the general practice being approximately one every two weeks), and planned and coordinated by the faculty members themselves.

A definite hour and day for all types of meetings should be established well in advance, allowing teachers time to organize class and personal schedules around these meetings. Some institutions have found it quite advantageous to schedule a majority of their general faculty meetings at least one full semester in advance, with provisions for additional or alternate dates in case of emergencies.

3. Faculty members or their representatives should be directly involved in the scheduling and planning of general staff meetings. This does not imply that administrative business is not be be included in the agenda; but if the purpose of these gatherings is merely to provide the opportunity for administrative reports, they should be labeled accordingly. In general, faculty meetings should be teacher-oriented and administratively coordinated rather than

administratively commissioned and operated.

Small staffs (with under 15 members) probably would be totally involved indirectly determining the agenda or planning the program for the over-all faculty meeting. However, when the number of teachers in a school is greater than this, group size may cause full faculty participation to become impractical and unwieldy. Large groups begin to consume valuable time of both teachers and administrators in working out program details with the principal. Consequently, either by administrative appointment or, preferably, faculty elections, representatives of the various grade levels, subject areas, or departments could serve on a faculty council. With the leadership and guidance of the administrator, this council could plan the agenda for the staff meetings. These teachers could then aid the principal in orienting this type of meeting toward educational problems and issues of concern and interest to the entire faculty.

It is also important to note that the function of such a council should not necessarily be limited to simply scheduling and planning general faculty meetings. This organizational pattern has great value in permitting teacher representation in many of the policy and regulatory matters directly affecting the teachers and their work. In schools where this plan has been used, high faculty morale and greater mutual respect between teacher and administrator were definitely noticeable.

4. An agenda for each meeting should be printed and distributed to all teachers at least one to three days in advance, with reminders of the date and time of the assembly appearing every day in the faculty bulletin for at least one week. Time limits for each gathering should be resolved beforehand and strictly adhered to. A maximum of one hour, includ-

ing the social phase, appears to be the commonly suggested practice. Research also indicates that these meetings are seldom held on Mondays or Fridays, because of the unusually busy schedules of teachers on those days. Although the smaller departmental, grade level, or subject area groups operate on a less formal basis, a minimum of two to three days' prior notice of these meetings is desirable.

These are but a few of the key factors to be considered in organizing and planning the general faculty meeting. If these meetings are cooperatively and purposefully planned, they can contribute significantly to the total educational program of a school. If not, they will simply serve as another intruding time-consumer in the already overloaded schedules of both teachers and administrators. One must remember that the purpose of any school program is to permit teaching and learning to take place. If any situation hinders either factor, a serious problem exists and must be corrected as soon as possible.

TEACHER EVALUATION: BARRIER TO COMMUNICATION?

Bertram C. Lindemann

Assistant Professor of Education
Montclair State College
Montclair, New Jersey

Kimball Wiles (among others) suggested that evaluation of teachers by supervisors is a barrier to effective communication between teachers and supervisors.[1] This notion has led many educators to recommend the removal of the evaluation responsibility from the hands of the supervisor in order to improve or facilitate communication with teachers.

The Problem

The assumption that evaluation acts as a barrier to communication between teachers and supervisors must be reexamined in the light of some new evidence collected by this author.[2]

Reprinted by permission from *Educational Leadership*, Vol. 28 (November, 1970), pp. 207-208.

1. Kimball Wiles. *Supervision for Better Schools*. Englewood Cliffs, New Jersey: Prentice-Hall, Inc., 1967, pp. 3-10.

2. Bertram C. Lindemann. "Communication Between Teachers and Supervisors." Unpublished doctoral dissertation, Department of Educational Administration, State University of New York at Buffalo, 1970, p. 49.

Hypothesis

Originally, it was thought that teachers who perceived that they were being evaluated by their supervisors would communicate less frequently with supervisors than would teachers who perceived that they were not being evaluated by their supervisors.

It was assumed, by Kimball Wiles and others, that evaluation was a barrier to communication; that is, that teachers viewed evaluation as a threat and, for that reason, would be rather reluctant to ask supervisors for advice for fear of inadvertently confessing their ignorance.[3]

Results

However, this did not prove to be the case after the data were collected and analyzed. Teachers and supervisors in two upstate New York public school districts were surveyed by mailed questionnaire. The results necessitate a restatement of the original assumption.

It was found that teachers who perceived that they are being evaluated by their supervisors communicated more frequently with their supervisors than did teachers who perceived that they were not being evaluated by their supervisors.[4]

Conclusion

Based on the findings, it may be assumed that teachers who perceive that they are being evaluated by their supervi-

---

3. George C. Homans. *Social Behavior: Its Elementary Forms*. New York: Harcourt, Brace & World, Inc., 1961, p. 334.

4. Lindemann, *op. cit.*

sors find it more rewarding to interact with supervisors than not to, in order to ingratiate themselves with supervisors and to assure themselves a good evaluation. And teachers who perceive that they are not being evaluated by their supervisors may not see a need to interact with supervisors.

Moreover, Unger assumes that ". . . the greater the degree of predictability between principal and teacher, the greater the willingness of the teacher to adopt trusting attitudes."[5] Unger defines trust as ". . . the mutual expectation and predictability persons have toward one another as they are developed through the social exchange process."[6]

It may be assumed that being evaluated is likely to be more predictable to teachers than not being evaluated. The more formal the evaluation, the greater the trust. The greater the trust, the more frequent teacher-supervisor interactions, according to the findings of another hypothesis in the author's study.[7]

Therefore, it is logical to assume that teachers who perceive that they are being evaluated by their supervisors are more likely to interact with supervisors than are teachers who perceive that they are not being evaluated by their supervisors.

Recommendations

A basic recommendation would be that supervisors ought to evaluate teachers. However, this recommendation, taken

---

5. Marvin H. Unger. "A Study of the Relationship of Selected Organizational Climate Variables and Personal Background Variables to the Expressed Willingness of Teachers to Adopt Trusting Attitudes." Unpublished doctoral dissertation, State University of New York at Buffalo, 1970, p. 17.

6. *Ibid*., p. 13.

7. Lindemann, *op. cit*., p. 49.

alone, would be incomplete without consideration of the methodology of evaluation employed as well as the rationale for having evaluation.

First, any evaluation of teachers ought to be a joint venture of supervisors and teachers. Teachers can be expected to be more accepting of evaluation results when they have had a part in developing the evaluation. This is a notion evolving from the concept of participative decision making.

Second, the focus of the evaluation should be the accomplishment of specific objectives stated in behavioral (operational) terms. The degree of effectiveness would be the measure of the discrepancy (if any) between what is expected (the objective) and what is accomplished (the behavior).

And, finally, the knowledge of the effectiveness would be the feedback the teacher needs to modify his course of action to align it with the stated objectives. This, after all, is the purpose of the evaluation.

TEACHER EVALUATION THAT MAKES A DIFFERENCE

Harold J. McNally

Chairman, Educational Administration
and Supervision
University of Wisconsin - Milwaukee

How to evaluate in education is one of our big, unanswered questions. Not that answers have not been given; they have been--hundreds of them. Most of these, however, are but partial answers, and many of them grossly oversimplify the questions. This is particularly true of those which apply to teacher evaluation.

A major difficulty in teacher evaluation is that we have not been able to get together on what we should be evaluating. Indeed, we do not even seem to be able to agree on why we evaluate teachers. With these two strikes against us, it is small wonder that we cannot achieve any consensus on how teachers should be evaluated. Whereas the variety of opinions on these matters is interesting, it is also confusing to practitioners in the field. The thesis proposed in this paper is that most efforts at teacher evaluation are far too narrowly focused, too oversimplified; consequently they omit important factors that are critical in improvement of teaching.

Reprinted by permission from *Educational Leadership*, Vol. 29 (January, 1972), pp. 353-357.

What Purposes?

There will be small argument, if any, that the purpose for which evaluation is undertaken will strongly influence what we decide to evaluate, and how we go about evaluating it. The purposes for which we evaluate teachers are manifold. Generally, we can divide the purposes of teacher evaluation into two categories: administrative and instructional. Each of these includes sub-categories. For example, administrative evaluation may be undertaken to decide whether or not a teacher will be employed for the next year, or whether he will be placed on tenure.

Many school systems have evaluated teachers to make decisions about what their salaries will be for the following year. These are so-called merit salary plans, which have almost always turned out to be unsatisfactory. Sometimes evaluations are used to make decisions about teacher transfers or promotions. All these are examples of evaluations for primarily administrative purposes; they are designed to gather information which is likely to help administrators to make administrative decisions. Some administrative evaluation is necessary, of course, and continually greater emphasis is being placed upon it because of the current growing emphasis on accountability.

Quite different, although closely related, is the instructional evaluation, that which has as its primary purpose the improvement of the teaching and learning program. Of course, we can all think of instances in which firing a teacher (or even a principal, for that matter) would help greatly in that respect. What is referred to here, however, is evaluation that is done with the hope that somehow it will result in better teaching and learning or, to broaden it out a little, better education. It is on this that we shall "zero in" for the remainder of this paper.

Four Views on Evaluation

There are at least four views of how evaluation can bring about educational improvement. First, there is the view that the very fact that teachers are evaluated motivates them to do a better job. There is, perhaps, a modicum of truth in this. Most human beings need a little goading, a little pressure, a little urging to exert themselves to perform more than adequately.

The fact that a teacher will be graded "excellent," "satisfactory," or "poor," however, will work no magic in this respect. For a teacher to change or improve, he needs to know how to change, to know what the changed teaching behavior looks like, to know what he is doing that is less than satisfactory, and what would be better. Just to be evaluated will not in itself provide the teacher with this help.

Second, therefore, are those who believe that evaluation should be for the purpose of helping the supervisor to teach the teacher how to teach better. Again, there is some validity in this. It is particularly applicable in the case of new teachers who need help in basic techniques of classroom management and in adjusting to a new situation. For most veteran teachers, however, this concept of evaluation tends to lack validity. It is becoming progressively less valid as the curriculum becomes more complex and sophisticated, and as programs of teacher preparation improve.

Most veteran teachers probably know more about what they teach, and about how to teach at the age level of the pupils they teach, than do most of their principals or supervisors. Few principals can at the same time know how to help a primary grade teacher with the newer methods of reading, and the fifth grade teacher with the new math or the "process curriculum" in science. Even in such basic matters as classroom control and management, most principals know that they have veteran teachers on their staffs who could teach them a thing or two. The didactic approach to evaluation may have had validity in the days when most teachers had little more than a "high school normal" training course; even today it may be useful with very new or very poor teachers, but it is not the main road to better education.

A third viewpoint is that the purpose of evaluation should be to stimulate the teacher's own self-evaluation of his functioning. This, too, has some validity; more, probably, than the other two viewpoints. It has the virtue of recognizing that nobody but the teacher can improve or change himself. Others may help him to change, encourage him to change. Yet whatever change takes place in a teacher is of his own doing. It has to take place inside him, and will take place only when he decides it is important to change, when he perceives a need for change, and when he understands with some clarity what the nature of the change ought to be.

Recapitulation

Whereas all three of the foregoing conceptions include a part of "the truth," all three founder on the same fallacy: the belief that all that needs to be changed is the teacher. The quality of children's learning experiences depends only in part on the teacher. True, this may be the most important part, but it is still only a part, and that part depends upon and is strongly influenced by other factors.

The problem has some parallel with that of "improving" minority group children in the slums. These children are the product of their situation, and until the situation (including the schools, of course) is changed in important ways, those children's perceptions, values, and behaviors will not change very much. Less clearly, but nevertheless truly, the quality of children's classroom experiences depends not only upon the teacher, important as he is, but on the entire teaching-learning situation.

Let us summarize what has been said about different kinds of evaluation. If we accept the proposition that the most important purpose of evaluation is improvement of the quality of the learning experiences of children, we can place conceptions of evaluation in an ascending order of probable effectiveness.

First, there is evaluation which simply judges whether a teacher is good, bad, or indifferent, and leaves it at that. This is the least effective form of evaluation for improving instruction.

Second, we have the conception of evaluation as supervisory analysis of a teacher's strengths and weaknesses, which enables the supervisor to teach the teacher how to teach better. This has some validity at the level of simple classroom management skills and certain relatively simple teaching techniques.

Third, there are those who maintain that our answer is to get teachers to engage in rigorous self-evaluation, since only the teacher can change himself. This is true as far as it goes, but it goes not far enough. The teacher is only one of the factors which determine the quality and variety of the educational experiences children will have.

Fourth, and this is my thesis, evaluation which has as its objective the improvement of the quality of children's learning experiences should be a cooperative study of the entire teaching and learning situation. This includes the teacher, of course. Yet it also includes the children; the facilities; the materials available; the nature of the community and its implications for children's curriculum experiences; the conception of education held by the principal and his staff; the pupil evaluation, marking, and reporting practices used; the time schedule; the climate of operation and expectations developed within the school by the principal and his staff; and other factors which bear importantly on the problem of providing opportunities for worthwhile learning experiences for children. It is conceivable, for example, that to improve the quality of the educational experiences of the children in the East Bottomley School, the most important change needed is a change in the principal's conception of what good education is. This means, of course, that the principal of the East Bottomley School will have to engage in some self-evaluation himself.

Characteristics of a Good Program

Within the framework of this point of view, what are the characteristics of a good program of evaluation? Let us propose a list of questions that suggest what the program should be like.

1. Is the evaluation program cooperative? That is, do administrative and supervisory personnel work both with individual teachers in cooperative study of individual classroom learning situations, and with groups of teachers, working in grade-level or problem-centered groups? The emphasis here is on cooperative study rather than on unilateral, one-way evaluation.
2. Is evaluation focused on the situation, not the teacher alone? Are administrative procedures, expectations, and attitudes examined for the degree to which they help or hinder variety, experimentation, and the quality of the learning experiences teachers help children to have? Are the adequacy, variety, suitability, and accessibility of instructional materials appraised? Is the relevance of the curriculum to the nature and needs of these particular pupils carefully examined? Is the school and classroom arrangement flexible, cheerful, interesting? Is the teachers' classroom behavior warm and friendly, orderly and well-planned, sprightly and interesting? In other words, are we putting only the teacher under the magnifying glass, or are we studying a variety of the factors which influence or determine the quality of the children's learning experiences?
3. Is the evaluation diagnostic rather than judgmental?

Do we concentrate on finding out what elements of the situation are causing problems, restricting progress, encouraging or inhibiting experimentation and creativity, contributing to effectiveness, and why? Or do we content ourselves (as we too often do) with making a judgment, and letting it go at that?

4. Does the process employed help the teacher and the principal (or other supervisor) maintain and build personal and professional self-respect and self-image, as well as respect for each other? Too often the process has demeaned and humiliated the teacher, affronting his professional respect and dignity. If we wish to develop the image of teaching as a profession, we have to treat teachers as professionals--as fellow professionals, if you will. Indeed, the advent of collective negotiation bids fair to leave administrative and supervisory personnel little choice in this. We shall have to treat teachers as fellow professionals, or else. A better reason, however, is that it is psychologically the soundest way to achieve better education.
5. Does the process foster self-evaluation on the part of all involved? If we study all the elements in the situation, that must include ourselves. Unless we evaluate ourselves, and the manner in which we influence the situation for good or for ill, we shall not achieve self-improvement. This applies to principals and supervisors as well as to teachers. Of course, those who are perfect can ignore this one.
6. Does the nature of the evaluation encourage experimentation, creativity, variation? A program that evaluates the teachers on the degree to which they conform to someone else's conception of what good teaching is, will not be likely to encourage teachers to try new approaches. A premium will be placed on playing it safe.

7. Does the evaluation program result in a higher quality and greater variety of opportunities for learning experiences for children in the classroom? This, of course, is the payoff. Unless the evaluation program makes a difference in the classroom, we may very well question whether it is justified at all. The ultimate test of the evaluation is simply this: does it make a difference that it is good?

Some Necessary Considerations

The multitude of studies that have been made of teacher evaluation leave no question that the principal is the key person in the program. It is the rare school system where the principal is not the person most responsible for teacher evaluation. It follows, then, that principals are the people on whom the quality, the nature, and the effectiveness of the evaluation program depend most. More than any other group, it is in their power to improve evaluation programs.

Yet they cannot do this alone, any more than can a teacher. As with teachers, principals are but a part of an educational context. Role expectations of the central office authorities, for example, either severely hamper, or can facilitate, principals' or supervisors' efforts to develop effective cooperative plans and procedures of evaluation. Furthermore, the approach advocated here calls for expenditures of time and effort on the part of teachers. This requires both commitment on the part of teachers, and administrative recognition that the activities called for by such a conception of evaluation are properly to be considered a part of the teaching day.

Accountability is the current "in" word. Increasingly --and not unreasonably--educators are being asked to account for their stewardship. If handled well, this can have a most salubrious effect on the educational establishment. However, in our sudden efforts to mollify the public, let us be certain we do not oversimplify the problem; we have had enough of that.

Let us not fall into the old, old trap that it must be the teachers, alone, who shall be accountable, that they shall be the scapegoats for the shortcomings of the system, whatever those may be. Let us keep our vision wide-angled, and make certain that we appraise the influence of all factors that shape the effectiveness of the teaching and learning process in the schools, and the results which that process achieves. If we do, it is just conceivable that in the course of rendering our accountability, we may also substantially improve the learning experiences of the children in the schools.

THE PRINCIPAL AND THE INSTRUCTIONAL PROGRAM

James Curtin

Chairman, Department of Elementary Education

University of Minnesota
Minneapolis, Minnesota

and

Stanley Gilbertson

Elementary Curriculum Coordinator
Bloomington Public Schools
Bloomington, Minnesota

The basic premise of this essay is that the elementary school principal is, and must remain for the foreseeable future, a leader in curriculum and instruction. Certainly this premise is not startling to those who have been directly involved in the elementary school principalship, but it is perhaps more important now than ever before that this concept of the principalship be clearly understood.

There appears to be a tendency on the part of many involved in the "new administration"[1] to regard the elementary

---

Reprinted by permission from National Elementary Principal, Vol. 45 (September, 1965), pp. 53-55.

1. This term is used by William W. Wayson in the April, 1965 issue of National Elementary Principal. Hollis Moore dates the "new ferment" in school administration as beginning in 1947. See his chapter, "The Ferment in School Administration," in Behavioral Science and Educational Administration, Sixty-third Yearbook, Part II, National Society for the Study of Education, pp. 11-32.

school principal as an administrator _rather than_ as a supervisor or curriculum worker. In his address to the 1964 Annual Meeting of the National Department of Elementary School Principals, Roald Campbell stated unequivocally, ". . . you are administrators."[2] In the same address, he proclaimed that "you are not instructional experts."[3] Erickson indicates that "instructional supervision by the principal seems, then, to be less and less defensible in many schools; in addition, it is becoming less necessary."[4]

These are provocative views, to be sure, but provocative views are not necessarily accurate. Let us state and examine the converse of these views: elementary school principals _are_ administrators, but they are not _only_ administrators; elementary school principals are (or should be) instructional experts, and instructional supervision by the principal seems to be _more and more_ defensible and is becoming _more_ necessary.

The primary business of the elementary school is instruction. Russell says flatly that the elementary school is the basis of all education.[5] If these are statements of fact, it is inconceivable that elementary school principals should know less and less about the foundation of educational quality in the schools of the nation. Others share our view that the elementary school principalship is central to instructional improvement. Dean and McNally, no strangers to elementary school educators, put it this way.

---

2. Roald F. Campbell, "Application of Administrative Concepts to the Elementary Principalship," _National Elementary Principal_, Vol. 44 (April, 1965), p. 22.

3. _Ibid._, p. 23.

4. Donald A. Erickson, "Changes in the Principalship," _National Elementary Principal_, Vol. 44 (April, 1965), p. 19.

5. James E. Russell presents an eloquent elaboration of this statement in Chapter 4 of _Change and Challenge in American Education_. Boston: Houghton Mifflin Company, 1965.

> It is true that other administrators should be familiar with the general purposes and nature of the elementary school program; but the elementary school principal needs to know that program as a physician knows anatomy, as an integral, pulsing system, with its complex detail. He should know its objective; the content, scope, organization and sequence of its learning program; and the rationales underlying those features. He should be acquainted with the strengths and weaknesses of various programs and methods, with the characteristics of good instructional methods and materials, and with effective ways of bring about improvement in them.[6]

One could indefinitely extend the list of intelligent, alert, and experienced people who clearly see an important relationship between curriculum and instruction and the elementary school principalship.

Despite the fact that there are those who see the elementary school principalship moving away from curriculum and instruction, there is some evidence pointing in the other direction. Studies done at the University of Minnesota indicate that superintendents, principals, members of boards of education, and the public expect the elementary school principal to be active in instructional affairs.

Schmaus found, for example, that 95 per cent of professors of education, 80 per cent of laymen, 94 per cent of teachers, and 95 per cent of superintendents in his sample regarded the principal's ability to recognize effective teaching as being "very important." While 4 per cent of the laymen in his sample regarded this ability to be of "no importance," none of the professional workers agreed with them.[7]

---

6. Harold J. McNally and Stuart E. Dean. "The Elementary School Principal," in _Preparation Program for School Administrators_ (Edited by Donald J. Leu and Herbert C. Rudman). _East Lansing_: Michigan State University, 1963, p. 117.

7. Roger Schmaus, "A Survey Study Examining the Opinions Held by Laymen, College Professors, Teachers, and Superintendents as to What an Elementary School Principal's Preparatory Program Should Be." Unpublished master's paper, University of Minnesota, 1959.

When Duneer and Skov investigated the perceptions of professors of education and school superintendents about the duties of elementary school principals, there was perfect agreement between their rankings: supervision was felt to be the most important duty and curriculum work ranked second.[8] Zimmerman's study found that elementary school principals felt that providing supervisory help was important, but professors of educational administration regarded the giving of such help as crucial to the principalship.[9]

The Fallacy of "Limited Knowledge"

We said earlier that the basic task of the elementary school is instruction, and that those who have a basic responsibility for the school--the principals--should know more and more rather than less and less about this basic task. Those who feel that there is "too much to know," that principals "can't keep up with everything," use this as an excuse for knowing nothing about curriculum and instruction.

Every complex endeavor imposes cruel demands upon those charged with its development. This is, and ought to be, a challenge for those involved. One may not know everything about curriculum content, but he may know a great deal and he can continue to learn. He should not be disqualified from participating in the instructional program simply because his knowledge does not extend to the farthest limits. In this limitation he keeps splendid company. No physician knows "all" medicine; no lawyer knows "all" law; and no

---

8. Virgil Duneer and Kenneth Skov, "A Study Comparing the Attitudes of School Superintendents with Those of Professors of Education in the Selection and Preparation of Elementary School Principals." Unpublished master's paper, University of Minnesota, 1959.

9. Roger Zimmerman, "A Survey of the Duties of Elementary School Principals in Minnesota." Unpublished master's paper, University of Minnesota, 1959.

physicist knows "all" physics. Even within highly specialized professions (and we hold that the principalship is highly specialized) members suffer from lack of knowledge. It is this realization that makes for the spirit of inquiry which inhibits arrogance. In other words, we reject the implication that if one does not know all, he knows nothing.

Why Principals Can Participate in Instruction

Let us turn to matters that indicate that well-educated and experienced elementary school principals can participate effectively in instruction and, in fact, serve as instructional leaders--a term derided by some members of the "new administration."

First, the elementary school principal has completed a four-year undergraduate major in elementary education. Second, he has had teaching experience in elementary schools. Third, he has completed graduate training in elementary education, including curriculum, supervision, psychology, and administration. Fourth, he serves in an educative milieu as a principal. Each of these elements of his pre-service, in-service, and experiential training has qualified him for membership on the instructional team.

What is sometimes overlooked is the fact that instructional leadership implies a great deal more than knowing the content of curriculum, important as this is. There is also the problem of leadership function as it relates to the improvement of learning. Various theories of administration deal with such things as nomothetic and idiographic approaches, decision-making processes, and organizational equilibrium, among others. It is becoming more clearly recognized that leadership is multidimensional, that the leader uses a skillful versatility in resolving conflicts, promoting cohesiveness with and among groups so that clearly identified goals may be achieved.

Now we come to the nub of the problem. What goals? Remember that the crucial function of the school is instruction, and it follows that leadership will be concerned with this primary goal. Is it too obvious to point out that the leader should understand these goals and how they are to be achieved? The processes of goal fulfillment must be as clearly understood as our present limited knowledge about them permits. About equally important is substantive knowledge of the nature of the goal.

Perhaps an example will illustrate what we mean. An overriding concern in every superior elementary school is the quality of reading instruction. The most obvious goal of reading instruction is to teach children to read with comprehension at rates appropriate to the material. If the leader is to move along the institutional line (the nomothetic approach) or the personal line (the idiographic approach) or both, then to what end? The process itself is not sufficient. He must be informed about what he needs to accomplish by these means and he must be informed about the field of reading to do it. If the leader regards decision making as his theory touchstone, one legitimately might ask, decisions about what? In order to accomplish the goals of reading instruction, do we use a phonic approach, the linguistic approach, the ITA? Is the individual approach more suited to our needs? If not, what basal readers should be use? These decisions are crucial, and in order to lead a group to sound decisions, the leader must be informed about the nature and consequences of the alternatives.

Not the Principal, Who?

Now we come to perhaps the most important question of all. If the elementary school principal does not take the responsibility for instructional improvement in his building, who will?

In the brave new world of the new administration, this

question is not dealt with adequately. Some see separate instructional teams carrying this responsibility. Others see a sort of "self-repairing" school organization. Still others envision large numbers of consultants or system-wide supervisors who will carry on the task of instructional improvement.

These alternatives are not adequate. Who, for example, initiates and develops a team-teaching program in a school? Who is responsible for seeing that evaluation is built into such an effort? Are these functions not the responsibility of the principal as an instructional leader? Organizational patterns alone will not insure better instruction, although some may increase its probability. Highly specialized supervisors may tend to drive curriculum areas farther apart, not bring them more closely together--unless an overview of the total supervisory service in a school is an operating part of the principal's job. This point cannot be overemphasized; it is the principal whose vantage point enables him to see all of the various aspects of the school program in its totality.

The point we make is that if the elementary school principal does not assume the responsibility for developing and improving curriculum and instruction in his building, no one else will.

At this point we must correct an implication that we may have unwittingly made. No matter how well educated, dynamic, and versatile an individual elementary school principal may be, he will need help. This help must come from all of his professional colleagues--administrative, supervisory, and teaching. It will need to come from parents of his school community and from social agencies within the community. This help, freely given and gratefully accepted, increases the principal's responsibility to his constituents because it makes his position the focal point, the integrative center, for those activities which will further the purposes of the school.

We do not claim that the elementary school principal is

a "one man team," but we do claim that he is a central member of the instructional team. Without his informed leadership, teaching, learning, and curriculum practice will be less effective.

THE SUPERVISOR LOOKS AT THE PRINCIPAL

Lillian I. Mosher

Supervisor of Elementary Education
Portland Public Schools
Portland, Oregon

In American education exciting and challenging things are taking place. One of the most encouraging things is the shift in focus to the elementary school.

This change of emphasis, the social and cultural revolutions, and the rapid technological advancements present important implications and complex demands for the elementary school principal.

Expectations Differ

In the analyses by theorists and researchers, there is limited agreement as to what the role of the elementary principal should be or how he should perform his role in dealing with the new demands.

Many provocative ideas have been proposed to define and to modify the changing role of the principal.

Erickson predicts "that the instructional supervision component of the principal's role will rather steadily lessen in importance as the principal's responsibility for stra-

Reprinted by permission from Educational Leadership, Vol. 23 (May, 1966), pp. 648-651.

tegic coordination is given increased emphasis."[1]

Curtin and Gilbertson insist that the principal is not only an administrator but "that the elementary school principal is, and must remain for the foreseeable future, a leader in curriculum and instruction."[2]

Greig and Lee suggest that a transformation of the principalship is timely and propose cooperative administration as a means for the improvement of the principalship. They make the analogy that, "If cooperative effort by teachers improves the effectiveness of planning, teaching, and evaluation, then the effectiveness of planning, supervision, and evaluation activities of principals might also be improved by collaboration."[3]

Applying the rationale behind team teaching, Anastasiow and Fischler propose "that the teaming of principals would be equally effective and help to meet some of the problems in elementary school administration."[4]

Cunningham considers the need to develop programs of continuing professional education crucial for the elementary principal and suggests that each state "create a commission on continuing education."[5]

Many and varied ideas have been suggested as future courses of action in view of ever-increasing demands. Some persons speak in fear that the public schools will not sur-

---

1. Donald A. Erickson, "Changes in the Principalship," National Elementary Principal, Vol. 44 (April, 1965), p. 20.

2. James Curtin and Stanley Gilbertson, "The Principal and the Instructional Program," National Elementary Principal, Vol. 40 (April, 1965), p. 53.

3. James Greig and Robert R. Lee, "Cooperative Administration," National Elementary Principal, Vol. 44 (January, 1965), p. 73.

4. Nicholas J. Anastasiow and Abraham S. Fischler, "A Proposal for Teaming Principals," National Elementary Principal, Vol. 44 (November, 1964), p. 60.

5. Luvern L. Cunningham, "Continuing Professional Education for Elementary Principals," National Elementary Principal, Vol. 44 (April, 1965), p. 66.

vive unless educational processes keep pace with the changing society; some perceive the role of the principal as a diminishing one. Some see increasing difficulty for the principal in maintaining status as an instructional leader; yet others see his future role as a challenging assignment.

How Fast Can the Principal Run?

What of today? We are living in what Kelley so aptly describes as a "moving, changing, becoming-but-never-arriving world . . ."[6]

Since the beginning of public education, the schools have changed to meet the demands of the times. Similarly, as conditions required more effective leadership, the principal modified his leadership functions to meet the complexity of his role.

That the present requirements of the elementary principal are a source of frustration is of common agreement. To be a skilled administrator of a school requires myriad competencies. It is doubtful that any organization demands as many diversified tasks of an individual. In an effort to meet changing demands, the elementary principal appears to be in much the same situation as Alice in Carroll's *Through the Looking Glass*.

Alice and the Queen had been running as fast as they could for some time. As they stopped to rest, Alice looked about in great surprise. She said, "Why, I do believe we've been under this tree the whole time! Everything's just as it was!"

"Of course it is," said the Queen. "What would you have it?"

"Well, in 'our' country," said Alice, still panting a

---

6. Earl C. Kelley. "The Fully Functioning Self," *Perceiving, Behaving, Becoming*, Arthur W. Combs, ed. Washington, D.C.: Association for Supervision and Curriculum Development, 1962, p. 10.

little, "you'd generally get to somewhere else--if you ran very fast for a long time as we've been doing."

"A slow sort of country!" said the Queen. "Now, here, you see, it takes all the running you can do to keep in the same place. If you want to get somewhere else, you must run at least twice as fast as that."

Who are those principals who "get somewhere"? What distinctive qualities do they possess?

Characteristics of a Good Principal

The effectiveness of the principal can be defined only in relation to the children, to the teachers, to others with whom he works, and to the community.

The following examples of effective leadership in the schools and in the community may serve to point up some traits of the participating principal.

In School A, many of the teachers are or have been involved in activities pertaining to curriculum improvement by serving on various curriculum committees with central office supervisors. The principal also serves on a curriculum committee. When asked how he promotes teacher participation, he replied:

> I believe involvement, not involvement for involvement's sake, but participation for a purpose increases interest and enthusiasm. This helps change attitudes.
>
> The hard work and extra hours I have spent on curriculum committees have resulted not only in a better understanding and greater knowledge, but I feel I'm a part of what is taking shape, I'm excited about it, and I want to share it.
>
> I don't pressure teachers to get involved. When a teacher works on a committee, the staff here plans ways in which that teacher can pass on information to others in the building. Enthusiasm is contagious and perhaps it's this sharing that opens the door for others to venture. We have a good time exchanging ideas that may benefit Mary or Johnny or Susan.

School B is experimenting with ways to create a good attitude toward reading in which two teachers form a leadership team. They use supervisors and librarians in a number of ways. The principal reads a wide variety of books and is able to talk enthusiastically with children in any classroom about many books at their level. He "pops" in and out of classrooms frequently to show a new book he has discovered, to remark about a character in a book, to get responses about books from children. He is a constant reminder of the value of books. His office! He collects books, all kinds of books, and the collection overflows the capacity of his bookcases. Children delight in selecting a special book from the collection on the floor. Books are for now. It takes time to obtain a bookcase.

The principal in School C has been well liked by every school community in which he has been assigned. Why was this so? He answered a question about his success in this way:

> Maybe you could call me selfish. I try to find out how my colleagues operate, and I "pick their brains" for specific techniques that I can use. I've found out that little details are important.
>
> We are all interested in children or we wouldn't be in this work. This seems so obvious that too often we fail to give oral confirmation of it to parents. I suppose in the busy schedule of doing we take for granted that our daily actions convey this message.
>
> Perhaps what success I may have with the school community is due, in part, to the mental notebook I keep. I try to make contact and really observe as many individual children as possible, and I file mental notes about each one. In this way I have a fund of information, and can share specifics of a positive nature with parents.
>
> The teachers here are doing a fine job of careful observation. We feel this concentration on actions and reactions has given us insights for better ways to help each child.

A Creative Role

A close look at these examples reveals some common threads:

> The principal's attitudes become the school's attitudes.
> The principal's strengths are reflected in the strengths of the school.
> The principal seeks and cooperates with other people in attaining goals.

What then, are the characteristics of a good principal? From observations in many schools, the "good" principal seems best to fit the conclusions Kelley draws from the behavior of the fully functioning person:

> The fully functioning personality thinks well of himself.
> He thinks well of others.
> He therefore sees his stake in others.
> He sees himself as a part of a world in movement--in process of becoming.
> The fully functioning personality, having accepted the ongoing nature of life and the dynamic of change, sees the value of mistakes.
> The fully functioning self, seeing the importance of people, develops and holds human values.
> He knows no other way to live except in keeping with his values.
> Since life is ever-moving and ever-becoming, the fully functioning person is cast in a creative role.[7]

To the degree that leadership in the schools exemplifies these characteristics, to that same degree schools will become humanizing centers for learning.

---

7. Ibid., pp. 18-20.

Index

INDEX